Journal of Biblical Literature
Monograph Series, Volume IX

A STUDY OF THE LANGUAGE OF THE BIBLICAL PSALMS

by

MATITIAHU TSEVAT

WIPF & STOCK · Eugene, Oregon

Wipf and Stock Publishers
199 W 8th Ave, Suite 3
Eugene, OR 97401

A Study of the Language of the Biblical Psalms
By Tsevat, Matitiahu
Softcover ISBN-13: 978-1-6667-3402-7
Hardcover ISBN-13: 978-1-6667-2943-6
eBook ISBN-13: 978-1-6667-2944-3
Publication date 8/13/2021
Previously published by Society of Biblical Literature, 1959

This edition is a scanned facsimile of the original edition published in 1959

PREFACE

The present study is the revised form of a doctoral
thesis submitted to the faculty of the Hebrew Union College-
Jewish Institute of Religion in the spring of 1953. It was
not without some hesitation that the writer embarked on an
attempt to make a small contribution to the research into
that book of the Hebrew Bible which has probably been
accorded the most study. He might not have carried through
his undertaking, had it not been for the constant encouragement
and advice of Professor Sheldon H. Blank. It is also in this
place that he expresses his deep indebtedness to Professor
Blank.

To Professor William F. Stinespring, the editor of
the Monograph Series, the author is very grateful for his
most valuable suggestions and the great interest he took in
the preparation of the manuscript.

Finally, the writer's cordial thanks are due to his
friends Professor Hillel A. Fine, Mrs. Fanny Berg, Mrs. Natalie
Mintz, and Mr. Max A. Shapiro for their suggestions of many
improvements in expression, and to Mr. Isaac Jerusalmi for
his meticulous care in typing the difficult manuscript.

M. T.

Cincinnati, August 1954

iii

TABLE OF CONTENTS

ABBREVIATIONS

The abbreviations for the periodicals are the common
ones; they are given as in R.H. Pfeiffer, Introduction to
the OT, 1941, pp. 842-844, in A. Lods, Histoire de la littérature hébraïque et juive, 1950, pp. 7 f., or in the individual commentaries of the Handbuch zum AT, ed. O. Eissfeldt,
1934 ff. In addition, the following abbreviations are used:

ARM   Archives Royales de Mari (publ. Imprimerie
        Nationale), 1951 ff.

BH   Biblia Hebraica, ed. R. Kittel, 3rd (ff.) ed.

EA   The El-Amarna Tablets, numeration of J.A. Knudtzon

Frdr J. Friedrich, Phönizisch-punische Grammatik
        (Anal. Orient. 32), 1951

GB   W. Gesenius, Hebräisches...Handwörterbuch...,
        16th (ff.) ed., F. Buhl, 1915 (ff.)

GK   Gesenius' Hebrew Grammar...ed...by E. Kautzsch,
        2nd English ed. by A.E. Cowley, 1910

GuBe H. Gunkel - J. Begrich, Einleitung in die Psalmen,
        1933

GuPs H. Gunkel, Die Psalmen, 1926

Har   Z.S. Harris, A Grammar of the Phoenician Language
        (Am.Or.Ser. 8), 1936

LVT   L. Köhler (-W. Baumgartner), Lexicon in Veteris
        Testamenti libros, 1948 ff.

1 QIs[a] First Isaiah Scroll from the first Qumran Cave
        (The Dead Sea Scrolls..., ed. M. Burrows, 1950)
REN   W. Rudolph, Esra und Nehemia, 1949
Sl   N. Slouschz, Oṣar haketovot hafenikiyot
        (Thesaurus of Phoenician Inscriptions), 1942
UH   C.H. Gordon, Ugaritic Handbook (Anal. Orient. 25),
        1947
VT   Vetus Testamentum

CHAPTER I

AIM AND METHOD

Biblical scholars first became interested in the
investigation of the language of particular parts of
biblical literature through higher criticism. Differences
in vocabulary, grammar, and style have been one of the
foundations for the theory of the separation of the Pentateuch into four documents. These studies were conducted
chiefly at the end of the past and the beginning of the
present century.[1] This linguistic approach has been applied
to other critical problems, too, e.g. Deutero and Trito
Isaiah[2] and Ezra.[3] Inquiries of this kind have contributed
greatly to our awareness of the existence and the essence
of various types of biblical Hebrew. But the interest in them
has been confined to areas where they can be used as an adjunct
to literary analysis. What enables their authors to differentiate one document from another or a few others is recorded
and evaluated. Where interdocumental differentiations cannot
be established or are of slight importance for the critical
aim, the interest of the student in linguistic investigations
diminishes.

Another feature, common to most of the linguistic

studies of parts of the Bible, is their concentration on those parts which are utterances of distinct personalities, such as the prophets, Ezra, the Chronicler. The linguistic approach of Pentateuchal criticism belongs here, too, since the activity of great personalities, standing at the beginning of a chain of tradition, is assumed. All these investigations have as their object the individual style of an outstanding personage or, at least, his style and its impact on the style of his followers; so strong was this influence that possible distinctions between his speech and that of his followers usually evade the eye of the modern critic.

The present study, an investigation of the language of the biblical psalms, has no primary aim beyond itself. Its object is a description of the idiom of the psalms as against the whole of classical Hebrew. After this objective has been reached, some of its aspects will be related to the history of psalm composition in Israel. The fact that only part of what is presented in the delineation of "psalm language"[4] is used for the historical investigation makes it clear enough that that investigation is not the aim of this study as a whole. Nor has that investigation been allowed to influence the method of the whole study. All that is being done in its descriptive part is done solely sub specie linguae.

Furthermore, this study is different from comparable

inquiries in that it is typological rather than individualizing. Its object is the idiom of a literary species.[5] The knowledge of the style of an individual may be helpful in understanding him fully, but will not be adduced to demonstrate that he really lived. The idiom of a literary species, on the other hand, is one of its constituents. A historic entity which is related to values is a free creation of the human mind. The Italian Renaissance did not exist until Jakob Burckhardt created it in his works. The _Gattungen_ of the biblical psalms came into being by the research of Hermann Gunkel.[6] It is, therefore, self-evident that the definition or accurate description of a maximum of elements of such a historic entity is of the highest importance. In view of these basic consider-ations, it is all the more astonishing that, to my knowledge, the language of the biblical psalms, wisdom literature, eschatology etc. has not had the benefit of special investiga-tions. At best one may find scattered remarks in general treatises or in commentaries. Besides the intrinsic linguistic value of such investigations, the hope is not altogether unfounded that they may make some contributions to the classifi-cation of the various literary _genres_ of the Bible whose nature and extent are still a matter of discussion.[7] Therefore, what-ever I may be able to say about the language of the psalms is a contribution to our better understanding of the literary species of the psalmic literature, of its basic means of expression, of the role of the pattern in it, and of its place

in the history of the civilization of Israel. Only some of
these details need elaboration and special examination in the
course of this study. Once light has been shed on possible
wider formal implications of such linguistic investigations,
the reader will draw in the data, small and dry like sand
grains, his own circles.

Finally, it is necessary, in opposition to many
philological studies, to adopt firm rules for collecting and
admitting the linguistic material for this investigation.
In the following paragraphs the rules will be set forth and
the method developed.

It goes almost without saying that an inquiry into
any aspect of the biblical psalms is not limited to the Psalter.
Defining a psalm as a devotional poem, man's address to God
in metrical form,[8] and including psalm fragments in the
investigation, lead to a principle which enables us to select
chapters and verses. Yet, it must be admitted that its
handling is not always easy and some results are open to
discussion.

The following are the psalms and psalm passages on
which this study rests: The Book of Psalms, exclusive of
ch.45, which is not a psalm, and the headings of the single
psalms. Further, Gen (9.26) 14.20; Ex 15.2-18; Dt.32.3 f.;
33.2-5; Ju 5.2-5, 31aα; 1 Sam 2.1-10; 1 Ki 8.12 f.; Isa 6.3;
12; 25.1-5, 9; 26.1-19; 33.2, 20; 38.10-20; 42.10-12; 44.23;

(51.9 f.) 59.(9-)12(-15a); 63.7-64.11; Jer 10.24; 11.18-20;
(12.1-3) 14.7-9, 19-22; 15.11, 15-18; 16.19; 17.12-18;
18.19-23; 20.7-13; 31.18 f.; Joel 1.19 f.; 2.17; (Am 7.2, 5)
Jonah 2.3-10; Mi 7.14-20; Na 1.2-8; Hab (1.2-4, 11b-17)
3.2(3-19); Job 7.7-21; 9.27-31; 10.2-22; 13.20-14.22;
30.19-23; Lam 1.9b-11, 20-22; 2.20-22; 3.19 f., 23, 43-45,
55-66; 5.[9] The parenthesizing of references indicates that
some uncertainty remains as to whether the passages are
devotional addresses to God, while the absence of parentheses
does not necessarily imply the absence of any doubt.

The inclusion of the Job passages and the exclusion
of others from the same book need a word of comment. Included
are those parts where Job turns away from his companions and
speaks to God. To be sure, the accusations, lamentations,
and petitions are part and parcel of the whole book in spirit
as in diction, and share, therefore, the linguistic peculiarities of its author. But their close relation to the rest of
the book does not make them intrinsically different from
other psalms. Many a poem of the Psalter may be an equally
faithful expression of its author's thoughts, feelings, and
style, the difference being that we have no other sources for
them but that one psalm.[10] Conversely, hymnic descriptions
of God in Job and a number of similar passages in other
books[11] are not incorporated in this study. They are not
worship but, perhaps, quotations from hymns or, more frequently
and more likely, ornaments of speech patterned after real hymns.

Yet in order to recognize them as such, the <u>Gattung</u> of the hymns, or any other <u>Gattung</u>, or the psalms at large must first be accurately described. Since the present study is itself a contribution to the description of the species of the psalms, passages which can be recognized as psalms only after the species has been established by detailed description are not admissible material for primary inquiry. The definition of the psalms, underlying this investigation, may be recalled here: man's address to God in metrical form. - Moreover, the doubtful or disputable passages are relatively so few that their inclusion or exclusion does not affect this study to any notable extent.

Only the psalms of the Hebrew Bible are treated in this study. This excludes not only the Aramaic passages from Daniel but also the prayers contained in those portions of Ecclesiasticus which come from the Cairo Geniza. Provisional and incomplete investigation of the Cairo texts has aroused my strong suspicion of their authenticity. It seems to me that at least parts of the "Hebrew Ecclesiasticus" are retranslated from (different?) Aramaic translations.[12]

A knowledge of the distinctiveness of the language of the psalms can be obtained only by comparing it with the language of the rest of the Bible. An exact comparison on a broad basis can be conducted only by statistics. Statistics is the method of this study. A detailed explanation of that method now follows.[13]

Words, grammatical forms, and a few phrases which
occur comparatively often in the psalms are singled out as
the elements of psalm language. Each element is given a
number which is retained throughout the study. For the order
of homonyms LVT is followed, if not otherwise remarked.
Pausal forms are replaced by context forms.

The following standards have been set for this study:
A word, a form, or a phrase is considered an element of psalm
language (i.e., it is "comparatively frequent") if it occurs
three times in the psalms and nowhere else in the Bible; four
times in the psalms and once outside of them; five times in
the psalms and three times outside; eight times in the psalms
and seven times outside; and in comparable ratios for words
and forms which occur more often. In a few cases with more
than ten psalm occurrences, the numbers of psalm and outside[14]
occurrences are equal. But in the great majority of cases,
the proportion of psalm to outside occurrences is much larger.
Hapax legomena and dis legomena, pet furnishings of linguistic
investigations, are not covered at all. If a word is so rare
that it occurs only once or twice in the Bible, its occurrence
in one book and omission in another may be due to its uncommon-
ness. Had it really been part of the diction of an individual
or a literary species, it would not have been used so seldom.[15]
In statistics, more than in any other method, one must beware

of operating with too few examples. But also items of overall
frequent occurrences whose psalm to outside ratios are slightly
negative for cogent or understandable reasons[16] are not
accepted into the body of this study. The rigidity of the
standards is even more important than the scope of the counted
and compared material.[17]

The elements are grouped in several lists and each
element is immediately followed by the ratio of psalm to outside occurrences. The figure before the colon gives the
number of psalm occurrences; that after it the number in the
rest of the Bible.[18] Alternative figures, figures with
question marks or figures in parentheses show my inability
to come to a decision because of the uncertainty of the text,
ambiguity of the particular passage with regard to its literary
species, and similar reasons which are usually given in the
notes. In some cases,[19] the ratio does not refer to the
specific word but to the tendency to use that word (or any
word) in various grammatical or stylistic forms. Psalm
occurrences, except those of the few elements which occur
more than 40 times, are fully documented.

An element is counted no more than once when it occurs:
in identical or virtually identical passages;[20] in formulas;[21]
in refrains[22] or other formal repetitions;[23] in paronomastic
expressions.[24] If one element occurs in Ps 119 more than two
or three times, it is not fully counted, but "+n" is added to

the number of the occurrences in the rest of the psalms and
the amount of "n", i.e. the number of occurrences in Ps 119,
is given in a note.[25] Greatfrequency of a word in this psalm
often bears testimony to the author's inability to vary his
expression rather than to a genuine pertinence of this word
to the diction of the psalms in general. But with this
content and this form of the psalm given, the question may
legitimately be asked whether an even more gifted poet would
have been able to avoid monotony of language. On the other
hand, it would not be justifiable to ignore a psalm which is
longer than most of the single books of The Twelve.

The distinction made in this study between psalms and
the rest of the Bible allows no special place for prose prayers.
Yet it is not advisable to disregard them. Linguistically
and literarily they constitute a class by themselves which
includes the following passages: Gen 24.12-14, 27; 32.10-13;
49.18; Ex 18.10 f.; 32.11-13(31 f.); Nu 10.36;[26] 11.11-15;
12.13; 14.13-19; 16.22; 27.16 f.; Dt 3.24 f.; 9.26-29; 21.8;
26.5-10, 13-15; Jos 7.7-9; Ju 10.10, 15; (13.8) 15.18; 16.28;
21.3; (1 Sam 1.11; 7.6; 12.10) 2 Sam 7.18-29; (15.31; 18.28)
24.10, 17; 1 Ki (3.6-9; 5.21) 8.(15-21)23-53, 56-61; (10.9)
17.21; 18.36 f.; 19.4; 2 Ki (6.17, 20) 19.15-19; 20.3;
Jer 32.17-25; Ez 9.8; 11.13; Jonah 1.14; 4.2 f.; Dan 9.4-19;
Ezra (7.27) 9.6-15; Ne 1.5-11; 3.36 f.; (5.19) 9.5-37;
1 Ch 29.10-19; 2 Ch 14.10; 20.6-12. The number of occurrences

in prose prayers of an item follows the number of psalm
occurrences, e.g. 5 (i.e. psalm occurrences)+2 prose:2 (i.e.
outside occurrences). Thus those occurrences are kept out
of either total and have no bearing on considerations of whether
or not a given word, form, or phrase is an element of psalm
language.

In order to appreciate the ratios of the single
elements, we must bear in mind that the psalms represent only
about one twelfth of the Bible.[27] If one applied this proportion mechanically, ratios of elements such as 3:0 or 10:6
would have to be interpreted as 36:0 or 120:6. Of course,
different types of literature do not permit blind comparisons
of their vocabularies. Even if it should turn out that a great
part of the elements of psalm language does not betray the
slightest vestiges of thoughts and experiences from the world
of prayer, its significance should be evaluated with caution.
In any event, the nonapplication of the factor 12 is the
strongest device of safety; what is now 3:0 or 10:6 is really
and clearly psalm language.

Here some criticism is expected. Since the psalms are
poetry, their language should properly be compared with that
of biblical poetry alone and not with biblical Hebrew in
general. There would be some merit to such a procedure, but
practical deductions cannot be drawn from it. Since nonde-
votional poetry is part of the "rest of the Bible", a given

ratio, e.g. 8:5, means that against eight psalm occurrences there are at best five in nonpsalm poetry, mostly, of course, far fewer than five. On the other hand and for this very reason, the number of psalm elements which can be ascertained from the material and by the method of the present study would be much higher, and our idea of psalm language grossly exaggerated and distorted, were this study limited to Hebrew poetry. For it would be much rarer for the number of outside occurrences to be great enough in relation to psalm occurrences to disqualify a word, a form, or a phrase from becoming an element of psalm language.[28] That which under the present circumstances, i.e. despite the fact that the psalms are only a small fraction of the whole Bible, satisfies the standards of this inquiry, certainly belongs to the hard core of the idiom under investigation.[29]

Moreover, such a procedure is meaningless for all practical purposes. We can linguistically compare the psalms with biblical Hebrew at large, which is known. We cannot compare them with the language of biblical poetry which is unknown. Everywhere one finds vague allegations about poetical Hebrew, sometimes random assertions that this or that word occurs only in poetry, but we still do not know what this idiom is like and even whether there is such an idiom at all, except in so far as it can be determined by a few known syntactical phenomena. As a by-product of this study it will become apparent that some current views concerning the

"idiom of Hebrew poetry" need correction.[30] It is, therefore,
preferable to begin with inquiries into more limited sections
of biblical literature. On the other hand, the limits must not
be drawn too closely if the method is a statistical one, lest
the available material be too scant for statistical purposes.
This, in turn, often induces the student to lower his require-
ments of frequency of occurrence.

Finally, a remark about the textual basis of this
study. It would render the preparation and discussion of the
material excessively burdensome to make critical investigations
into the text of the several thousands of psalm and outside
occurrences referred to in the following lists. Nor is it
a peremptory requirement. With such a large amount of material
as the basis of the inquiry, characteristic phraseology is
as likely to be omitted as added in the process of textual
corruption. Nevertheless the text is critically appraised
quite frequently, and conjectures lead occasionally to changes
of the ratio.[31]

CHAPTER II

THE LANGUAGE OF THE PSALMS

I. LISTS

A. Words and Phrases

An inquiry into the language of the psalms naturally
makes word study its major objective. Besides the technical
reason for this concentration on one aspect of language, viz.
that for grammar and phraseology there is nothing as exhaustive
as a concordance or a detailed dictionary for the lexicographical field, there are other, inherent reasons. One
cannot expect major morphological differences between the
idioms of various types of biblical literature. The speaker
or writer may alter his vocabulary in a given situation, but
he can hardly apply another set of verbal prefixes without the
risk of speaking or writing unintelligibly. Nor does the
poetical structure of the psalms allow for the development of
a syntax appreciably different from other types of biblical
verse. The number of words in the hemistich, the usual syntactical unit of classical Hebrew poetry, is very small and,
within a given meter, rather rigid. This condensed speech
frequently contains the syntactical essentials alone. Sub-
ordinate clauses are rare, and subordinating conjunctions even

more so. All this restricts the possibility of syntactic
varieties. On the other hand, word order is so free that
there is hardly a standard from which deviations may be noted.
Finally, the use of the so-called tenses often escapes syntactical regulation. The course of the following investigation
is partly defined by these characteristics.

The lexicographical material will be presented to
begin with, and among it first those words, word forms, and
word groups which occur three times or more in the psalms
and nowhere else in the Bible.

1) אנף Qal 5+2 prose:0.[32]

2) √אפף 4:0.[33]

3) √גמר 5:0.[34]

4) (דּוֹבֵר(י) כָּזָב/שְׁקָר(ים), "lie teller(s)" 4:0.[35]

5) דַּךְ 3:0.[36]

6) דכה verb 5/6:0.[37]

7) זִמָּה 4:0.[38]

8) הִגָּיוֹן 3:0.[39]

9) הוֹלְלִים 3:0.[40]

10) זַלְעָפָה 3:0.[41]

11) יפע, "to appear, shine forth", with God as subject
5:0.[42]

12) יִרְאָיו of God 12:0.[43]

13) יִשְׁרֵי לֵב 7(8):0(1).[44]

14) כבוד שׂם/שׂמה 3:0.[45]

15) לֵב/רוּחַ נָכוֹן 5:0.[46]

16) כשש Piel, "cringe" 3:0.[47]

17) (לְכִסֵּא) , "(sit/install) on (a chair/throne)" 3:0.[48]

18) לחם I , "fight" Qal 4:0.[49]

19) מָגֵן divine epithet 3:0.[50]

20) סְבִיבוֹתָיו, סְבִיבָיו of God (his entourage) 6:0.[51]

21) סֹךְ epithet of the Temple (or part of it ? 42.5!) 3:0.[52]

22) סֶלַע divine epithet (always סַלְעִי) 3:0.[53]

23) סֵתֶר sensu religioso 7:0.[54]

24) ענה, verb with water or the like as subject and man as indirect object 4:0.[55]

25) עוֹדֵד Poel, Hitpoel 3:0.[56]

26) עֵדוּת (synonym of תּוֹרָה[57]) 5:0.[58]

27) עֹז , "refuge" (√עזז) 7(8?):0(1?, 2?).[59]

28) עטה (verb)+"shame" (כְּלִמָּה, חֶרְפָּה, בּוּשָׁה) 3:0.[60]

29) עָתָק 4:0.[61]

30) עֹשֵׂה פֶלֶא 5:0.[62]

31) פִּקּוּדִים , "commandments" 3+n:0.[63]

32) צמח Piel, Hiphil 11:0.[64]

33) קַצְוֵי אֶרֶץ 3:0.[65]

34) √רגש 3:0.[66]

35) רוּחַ קָדְשֶׁךָ/קָדְשׁוֹ 3:0.[67]

36) מִרְמוֹת (pl.) 3:0.[68]

37) רִשְׁעֵי אֶרֶץ 3:0.[69]

38) מִשְׂגָּב sensu religioso 10:0.[70]

39) שׁחק verb, with God as subject, and the wicked as object 3:0.[71]

40) מְצָרִים (followed by a substantival or pronominal genitive) 4:0.[72]

41) שׁוֹרְרִים, "enemies" (always שׁוֹרְרָי) 5:0.[73]

42) אָך (sing.) 3/4:0/1.[74] [75]

The second group comprises those words, forms, and word groups which occur both in the psalms (four times or more) and outside.[76]

43) אֵלִים, "god(s)" 4:1/2.[77]

44) אֱמוּנָה of God 22/23:1.[78]

45) אָמַר (sing.) 4:1(2?).[79]

46) אִמְרָה 6(7?)+n:8.[80]

47) אַפְסֵי אָרֶץ 8:6.[81]

48) אָרֶץ as a genitive of a group of people to indicate its universality 14:14.[82]

49) אַחֲרֵי־ with a substantival genitive 25:11.[83]

50) אַשּׁוּרִים(אֲשּׁוּרִים) 5(6?):3.[84]

51) בַּל 39:25.[85]

52) בְּנֵי אָדָם 15+1 prose:10.[86]

53) גֵּאִים 2+19 emendations:2.[87]

54) גֵּאוּת 5:3.[88]

55) גִּיל verb 20/18:20/22.[89]

56) גמל verb 10+1 prose:10.[90]

57) מָגֵן divine epithet 10:3.[91]

58) √דחה 6:2.[92]

59) I הגה <u>Qal</u> 12(13)/11:9/10(11).[93]

60) הֹוד וְהָדָר 4:1.[94]

61) II הַוָּה, "destruction" 8:4(6). The psalms prefer the pl. to the sing. 7:1.[95]

62) הֵיכַל קָדְשֶׁ/קָדְשׁוֹ 6:2.[96]

63) הלך <u>Piel</u> 15/14/13:10/11/12.[97]

64) זֵדִים 2+n+'2' emendations:4.[98]

65) זָכָר 13:10.[99]

66) זנה <u>Qal</u> 9:5.[100]

67) חיה ratio of <u>Piel</u> to <u>Hiphil</u>. In the psalms 11+n+1 prose:1; outside 31:21.[101]

68) II √חלץ, "save, be saved, withdraw" 9:4.[102]

69) חנן <u>Qal</u>; with God as subject 26:14[103]; with man as subject 4:9.[104] Other verbal stems 3+2 prose:8.[105]

70) חָסִיד 26:3.[106]

71) חֶסֶד of God 96+12 prose:27; of man 2:57.[107] Together 98+12 prose:84.[108]

72) חסה verb 25:8.[109]

73) מַחְסֶה divine epithet 11:1;[110] all meanings 14:7.[111]

74) יָּה 19:0/1.[112]

75) יחל <u>Piel</u> 9+n:9.[113]

76) יָמִין of God 19:4.[114]

77) יִרְאֵי יהוה/אֱלֹהִים 7:5.[115]

78) נִפְלָאוֹת, "miracles" and the like 5+1 prose:2.[116]

79) מִישָׁרִים ethical and juridical term 8+1 prose:7/8.[117]

80) כון <u>Polel, Polal, Hitpolel</u>; with God as grammatical

- or logical subject 13+1 prose:4;[118] with other subjects 7:6.[119] Together 20+1 prose:10.

81) מָכוֹן 6+3 prose:4.[120]

82) מוט Qal 8:6;[121] Niphal 16/17:5;[122] other verbal stems 1:1.[123] Together 25/26:12.

83) מַלְכֵי אָרֶץ 5:2.[124]

84) נבע Hiphil, "speak, pronounce" 6:2.[125]

85) נְדִיבִים (pl.) 8:6.[126]

86) נַחֲלָה. Israel is God's נַחֲלָה 13+4 prose: 12(13?, 14?, 15? 16?).[127]

87) I נֶצַח, "everlasting, forever" 22/21:16.[128]

88) סבב, distribution of perfect and imperfect over Qal and Poel, respectively. A. Perfect, a) Qal 9:12;[129] b) Poel 0:0. B. Imperfect, a) Qal 4:38;[130] b) Poel 8:3.[131] This shows that for the perfect the psalms prefer the Qal, for the imperfect the Poel. Other parts of the Bible use the Qal almost exclusively.

89) סתר Hiphil, with God as subject and man as object; idea: protection 5:1.[132]

90) סתר Hiphil (Niphal), with God as subject and his פנים as object; idea: anger 12:11/12.[133]

91) עֲדֵי־עַד 5:1.[134]

92) לָעַד 12:6.[135]

93) עוֹלָה 5/4+n:3.[136]

94) עֹז, "might" 43/42:(33?)34/35.[137]

95) II עטף Hitpael, "be feeble, faint away" 5:1.[138]

96) עֶלְיוֹן divine name or epithet of Israel's God 20:6.[139]

97) I עלל Poel, Poal, Hitpoel, "deal with" 5:2.[140]

98) עוֹלָם (adv.), לְעוֹלָם 70+3 prose:65[141]

99) לְעוֹלָם וָעֶד עוֹלָם וָעֶד 11:4.[142]

100) מֵעַתָּה וְעַד עוֹלָם 5:3.[143]

101) עַד עוֹלְמֵי עַד לְעוֹלָמִים עוֹלָמִים 7/6:4/5.[144]

102) √עלה √עלם √עלל. a) Verbs of all three roots 13/12:8/9;[145] b) √עלל as against the rest. √עלל 7/6:2/3; √עלה and √עלם together 8/7:16/17.[146]

103) פֶּלֶא, "miracle" 9:3.[147]

104) נִפְלָאוֹת, "miracles" 24+1 prose:9.[148]

105) פלט Piel, "save" 16/17:2.[149]

106) פעל verb 27:26.[150]

107) פֹּעַל 10(11):4,[151] פְּעֻלָּה 1:1,[152] מִפְעָל 1:1,[153] "work, deeds of God" Together 12(13):6.

108) פַּעַם, "foot" (always dual or, once[outside], pl.) 8:4(5).[154]

109) מְצוּלָה 8+1 prose:3.[155]

110) צוּר divine epithet 18:9.[156]

111) צִיץ (GB, LVT I צוּץ), verb "blossom" 5(4?):3.[157]

112) I צַר, "distress" 13:9/10.[158]

113) II צַר, "adversary, enemy" 30+1 prose:30/31.[159]

114) צוֹרֵר, "enemy" 12:5.[160]

115) קדם verb 12:10.[161]

116) קָדְשׁוֹ as genitive 20+1 prose:7.[162]

117) קום verb 23/21+1 prose:18/20.[163]

118) קָמִים (always pl.), "enemies" 6:2.[164]

119) בְּ ראה (הִבִּיט) +enemy, "to experience the enemy's misfortune" 6:1.[165]

120) רַבַּת adverb 5:2.[166]

121) רום Polel and Hiphil with God as subject and man as object; idea: salvation from danger or humiliation 8:2.[167]

122) רום verb+ קרן 10:1.[168]

123) רְמִיָה, "lie, treachery" 5/6:3/4.[169]

124) רְעִים, "wicked" 10:6.[170]

125) √שׂבר a) Piel, "to hope"; b) שֵׂבֶר, "hope" 6:2.[171]

126) שׂגב verb, "protect; be protected" 5:2(3?).[172]

127) שׂמן verb 5:1.[173]

128) שׂיח verb 9+n:4.[174]

129) מַשּׂוֹא 9:4.[175]

130) II√שׂוה, "make" 5/4:1.[176]

131) שַׁחַת 12:11.[177]

132) שְׁכֵנִים, "the (hostile) nations (in and) around Palestine" 4:1.[178]

133) מִשְׁפֶּן pl. in form with sing. meaning 5(4):2.[179]

134) אֵבֶל 19:13.[180]

135) תְּהוֹמוֹת (pl.) 11:3.[181]

Next come lists of words, forms and phrases with which it is not possible or not advisable to continue with the over-all alphabetic order. The first list deals with various formations of roots ישׁע and I עזז,[182] either alone or as part of particular phrases.

136) √יֵשׁע. The root is very frequent in the Bible in
general and in the psalms in particular.

A. The following substantives occur: יֶשַׁע 23/21:9/11;[183]
יְשׁוּעָה 45/44/43+1 prose:17/18/19;[184] יְשׁוּעוֹת 8:1;[185] [186]
מוֹשָׁעוֹת 1:0;[187] תְּשׁוּעָה 13:19.[188] The ratio of all five substantives together is 90/86+1 prose:46/50 which is not sur-
prising, since "salvation" and "help" are genuine concepts
of prayer. It is against the background of this overall
ratio of approximately 2:1 that the relative frequency of
יְשׁוּעוֹת (8:1) and the relative infrequency of תְּשׁוּעָה (13:19)
must be observed in order to obtain an awareness of what is
psalm language and what is not.[189]

B. a) The lengthened form יְשׁוּעָתָה is psalm language as
are the forms ending in תָה‎ in general. This will be shown
later.[190] Here it is noted that whenever the word meaning
"salvation" is preceded by ל + a substantive or a pronominal
suffix, it appears in the simple form יְשׁוּעָה, while whenever
it precedes them, it assumes the longer form יְשׁוּעָתָה; this
latter form is reserved solely for these specific cases.[191]
The same situation prevails with regard to עֶזְרָה and עֶזְרָתָה,
showing that this is not accidental.[192] b) In the phrase
"my/thy...God of Salvation"[193] which is psalm language
(12/11:2/3), the genitive is regularly יֶשַׁע (eleven times),
other substantives from √יֵשׁע are the exception (three
times).[194]

137) I √עָזַר a) Like No. 136 B. a) עֶזְרָה or עֶזְרָת is,
with one exception, preceded by לְ + a pronominal suffix,
while עֶזְרָתָה, a psalm word, is followed by לְ + a pronominal
suffix and is used only in this combination.[195] b) The
phrase " חוּשָׁה + to my help" is always composed with לְעֶזְרָתִי
(3:0),[196] never with לְעָזְרִי or a derivative from *√יׁשׁע

In this paragraph a list of words is drawn up for
"pray, praise, lament, entreat" etc. There is no need for
a special investigation to realize that those words are
numerous in the psalms. Yet of the following roots, not
all formations which are known from the Bible are used in
the psalms, while some are exclusively psalm property.
A clear illustration is No. 140. Furthermore, usage or
avoidance of some roots and forms will be considered in a
later chapter. [197] Here the list is given in order to continue with the presentation of the material as far as it has
come to my attention. The direct or indirect object of all
the active verbs, the subject of the passive verbs, and the
genitive of the substantives in this group is God.[198]

138) II ברך Piel 23:11/12;[199] Pual 0+2 prose:0.[200]
139) II √הלל[201] a) Verb. Piel 53+1 prose:14(23);
Pual 5:0(2);[202] Hitpael 0(7):0(13). b) הַלְלוּיָא 24:0.[203]
c) Substantives. מַהֲלָל 0:0(1); תְּהִלָּה 32(35):7(23).[204]
Together 114(124)+1 prose:21(62).

140) I √זמר a) Verb 39:0. b) Substantives I זָמִיר

2:0(1);[205] זִמְרָה 2:2;[206] מִזְמוֹר 0:57.[207]   Together 43:59(60).[208]

141) *אֶחָזוּן (only the pl. occurs) 8+3 prose:7.[209]

142) II √ידה a) Verb 59+14 prose:15.[210]   b)תּוֹדָה,
"thanksgiving" 7:3;[211]   a sacrifice 5:13;[212]   "confession"
0:2;[213]   "marching and singing band" 0:3.[214]   Together
71+14 prose:36.

143) רום Polel, Polal 9/10+1 prose:0.[215]

144) √רנן a) Verb. Qal 4:14/15;[216]   Piel, Pual (once)
20/21:5;[217]   Hiphil 3:2.[218]   b) Substantives:[219]   רִנָּה 16+1
prose:14;[220]   רְנָנָה 2:2.[221]   Together 45/46+1 prose:37/38.[222]

145) I√שבח   5:2.[223]

146) I√שוע a) Verb 13/12:9/10.[224]   b) שַׁוְעָה 7:3.[225]
Together 20/19:12/13.

147) שיר verb, excluding the participles שָׁרָה, שָׁר,
מְשׁוֹרֵר, meaning "singer".   Qal 27:8;[226]   Polel 0:2.   Together
27:10.

B. Grammatical Number of Words for
Musical Instruments

A survey is now being made of the use of the grammatical
number of words for musical instruments.   Our interest is
attracted by those cases where the words for lyre, harp etc.
stand for a chorus of lyres or harps of the Temple music.
Is the form of the sing. or of the pl. used for the collective?

148) כִּנּוֹר   sing. 8(11):3/4/5;[227]   pl. 0:14.[228]

149) נֵבֶל   sing. 4.(6/7):2/3;[229]   pl. 0:14.[230]

150) עֲשׂוֹר sing. 3:0; no pl.[231]

151) אַף sing. 3:2/3/4;[232] pl. 0:7.[233]

152) מְחֹלָה, מָחוֹל [234] sing. 4:3;[235] pl. 0:7.[236]

C. Grammar and Style

The following items show that the psalms are unique with respect to a few grammatical phenomena.

153) ־ֵנִי pronominal suffix 1st pers. sing. used with prepositions 4:0.[237]

154) ־ֵכִי, ־ֵיְכִי pronominal suffixes 2nd pers. sing. and pl. fem. used with substantives, prepositions, and verbs 10:(1+4 Ketivs=)5.[238]

155) ־ֵמוֹ, ־ֵימוֹ, ־ֵימוֹ pronominal suffixes 3rd pers. sing.[239] and pl. used with substantives and prepositions. a) With substantives ־ֵמוֹ 3:0;[240] ־ֵמוֹ 3:0;[241] ־ֵימוֹ 10:6;[242] b) אֲרִימוֹ 2:0[243] c) With prepositions לָמוֹ 29:26;[244] אֱלֵימוֹ 1:0;[245] עָלֵימוֹ 3:9.[246] Together 51:41.

156) ־ֵמוֹ/מוֹ pronominal suffix 3rd pers. pl. used with verbs 19:2.[247]

157) זֶה, זוּ, זוֹ determinative pronouns governing relative clauses. זֶה 5:4;[248] זוּ 12/11:2/3;[249] זוֹ 1:0.[250] Together 18/17:6/7.

158) ־ָה, ־ָתָה nominal endings with no terminative, locative or similar function. ־ָה 2:2/3;[251] ־ָתָה 10:3/4.[252] Together 12:5/6/7.

159) קוּמָה lengthened imperat. sing. masc. 116/117+18/14

prose:122/119.[253] The significance of these absolute figures,
which are almost equal one to the other, is greatly surpassed
by the import of the ratio within the psalms of קָטְלָה to קְטֹל
as compared with the corresponding outside ratio.[254] Psalms
116/117+18/14 prose:107/106+23/21 prose; outside 122/119:
960/959. In other words, the form קָטְלָה is relatively more
than eight times as frequent in the psalms as it is in the
rest of the Bible. Moreover, it occurs in the psalms more
often than the simple form קְטֹל .For the psalms, קָטְלָה is the
normal imperative.[255]

160) הֵמָּה אֹזֶךָ as against חַם אֹזֶךָ . We find הֵמָּה אֹזֶךָ
5+2 prose:0;[256] while חַם אֹזֶךָ 1:3.[257]

161) עָדֵי 7:4.[258]

162) מָאֹד word order; מָאֹד precedes the modified word
3:0.[259] (The ratio of the inverse order is about 30:270.)

The following list comprises a few stylistic phenomena.

163) וַאֲנִי/וַאֲנַחְנוּ as subject of a verbal sentence when
it refers to the psalmist. This emphasizes his difference
from, and his opposition to, the wicked or to his enemies
(usually the same persons) who are mentioned in the same verse
or immediately before. The ratio does not refer to the psalms
as against the rest of the Bible, but to those psalm passages
which follow this stylistic peculiarity as against those few
which do not, if there are any such. a) וַאֲנִי 15/14(13):0/1(2);[260]
b) וַאֲנַחְנוּ 4(3)+1 prose:0(1).[261] Together 19/18(16)+1 prose:0/1(3).

164) a) אֲנִי אָמַרְתִּי . a) וַאֲנִי אָמַרְתִּי ; b) אֲנִי אָמַרְתִּי b) 164)
4:0;[262] b) וַאֲנִי אָמַרְתִּי 3:5(6).[263] Together 7:5(6).[264]

165) Active and passive, or transitive and intransitive, of the same verb in close succession with God as subject of the active or transitive 8:1.[265]

166) That form of poetic parallelism which repeats rather than varies one or two words of the first _stichos_ in the parallel _stichos_ or _stichoi_ (a b c // a b d and the like) 30(32?)/29(30?):19(20?)/20(21?).[266]

II. ADDITIONAL LISTS

A. Words and Phrases of Substandard Frequency

It has been the essential requirement of this study to set rather severe standards for admission of words, forms, and phrases into the lists of elements of psalm language in order to delineate a clear picture of that idiom and to provide solid ground for the following discussions and such conclusions as may be drawn therefrom. Thus, much material has been excluded which, while not satisfying set standards, might be of interest to the student because of its relative frequency. Moreover, the philologist looks not only for sharp contours, such as statistics can provide, but also, by way of complement, for borderline cases and flowing transitions. Therefore, material will now be presented which does not conform to the standards set down for this study (referred to as "substandard material"). Because of the very nature of this material, it

cannot be hoped that the following list will be exhaustive.
In any event, no proof will be based on items contained in
this list. Hapax legomena are not included.

167) אֲזַי 3:0.[267]

168) אֵל (sing. and pl.) 81(79)+6 prose:126/127.[268] [269]

169) I אֲנָקָה, "sigh" 3:1.[270]

170) אֱנוֹשׁ 18+1 prose:22.[271] [272]

171) אֲרֶשֶׁת 1+'1'emendation:0.[273]

172) נָתַן פְּלִיוֹת וָלֵב or similar expressions 3:1.[274]

173) בָּעַר 3:2.[275]

174) גַּאֲוָה 7:11.[276]

175) גדל Piel 2:0.[277]

176) גוּר בְּאֹהֶל of God 2:0.[278]

177) I דבר Hiphil, "subdue" 2:0.[279]

178) דֹּרוֹת עוֹלָמִים, (לְ)דוֹר דֹּרִים, (לְ)דוֹר וָדוֹר, (לְ)דוֹר דּוֹר 19/18:23/24.[280]

179) דּוּמָה 2:0.[281]

180) הַבְלֵי שָׁוְא 2:0.[282]

181) הָגִיג 2:0.[283]

182) הֲלֹם 3:3.[284]

183) זִיז שָׂדַי 2:0.[285]

184) חֲיוֹ- (cstr.) 4:4.[286]

185) חֶלֶד 4(?):1.[287]

186) חלכה 3(2?):0.[288]

187) מַחְשָׁךְ 4:3.[289]

188) יְחִידָה, "soul" 2:0.[290]

189) יָיֵן 2:0.[291]

190) כָּבֵד (MT mostly כָּבוֹד), "liver" as organ of thinking and feeling 4:2.[292]

191) עַד מְאֹד 5+n:8/9.[293]

192) אֲמִתָּה 2:0.[294]

193) מחץ verb 5/4:7/8.[295]

194) √מיל (GB, LVT[II] √מול) 3:0.[296]

195) √מסה 3:1.[297]

196) מָנוֹס 4:4.[298]

197) √מעד 4:2.[299]

198) נָעִים 5/6:6/7.[300]

199) מַשּׁוּאוֹת (only the pl. occurs) 2:0.[301]

200) מַעְגָּל "track, course" 5:8.[302]

201) I עטף, "envelope(oneself)" 2:0.[303]

202) עטר verb 4:3.[304]

203) עֲלִילָה 10(+1 prose עֲלִילִיָּה):12.[305]

204) מִן הָעוֹלָם, מֵהָעוֹלָם, לְמִן עוֹלָם, מֵעוֹלָם 9+2 prose:12.[306]

205) עשׁן verb 4:2.[307]

206) עשׁשׁ verb 3:0.[308]

207) √פזר 5:5.[309]

208) פרק Qal, "rescue" 2:0.[310]

209) צָרָה 32/31+4 prose:36.[311]

210) קֶדֶר used as an adverb 3:1.[312]

211) מְקַהֵל(ה) 2:0.[313]

212) צֹאן(עַם)מַרְעִית of God, epithet of Israel 4:3.[314]

213) III רֵעַ or II רֵעָה, "intention, thought" 2:0.[315]

214) שְׂרַעַפִּים (only the pl. occurs) 2:0.[316]

215) מְשׁוֹאֹלוֹת (only the pl. occurs) 2:0.[317]

216) שַׁחַק, "cloud, sky" 8:10.[318]

217) שִׁית verb 36+1 prose:42.[319]

218) √תֵּאָב 3:0.[320]

B. Words and Forms Which Are (Virtually)
Absent from the Psalms

The following list is different from the previous ones.
Recorded here are not words or forms which do occur in the
psalms, but those which do not or are conspicuously rare.
If it is not easy to undertake the compilation of comprehensive
lists of items which do occur, it is precarious to embark on
even a sketchy composition of the second type. Since everything which is missing in the psalms cannot be noted, a selection
is to be made. How to select? Subjectivity seems unavoidable.
However, all our scruples and demurs do not change the fact
that a language is characterized by what is not in it as well
as by what is in it. The problem must be tackled. In order
not to let things get out of hand, narrow limits are delineated
and a few criteria established. Of two or more well attested
words or forms of identical meaning, the one which is missing
or conspicuously rare in the psalms is recorded in the case of

A. One of two different stems of the same verb;

B. One of two or more different nominal formations of
the same root;

C. One of two words differing from each other in one

phoneme only;

D. One of two or more not formally qualified synonyms which is, as a rule, exceedingly frequent in the rest of the Bible.

These criteria make it clear, but it may be stated explicitly, that in no case does the content have an influence on the presence or the absence of any one of those words and forms inside or outside the psalms. It need not be stressed that the profile of psalm language will stand out more sharply at those points where its elements can be held against the background of their synonyms of the following list. At a later stage of this study it will become apparent what further use can be made of this list.

A. a) אנף Hitpael 0:6; cmp. 1) אנף Qal 5+2 prose:0.

b) II עטף Qal, Niphal, Hiphil 1:6;[321] cmp. 95) II עטף Hitpael 5:1.

c) I עלל Hitpael 0:6;[322] cmp. 97) I עלל Poel, Poal, Hitpoel 5:2.

B. d) ישׁר 2+1 prose:13;[323] cmp. 79) מישׁרים 8+1 prose: 7/8.

e) Derivations from $\sqrt{\text{ישׁע}}$ and their usage. See the detailed differentiation in No. 136.

f) Derivations from I$\sqrt{\text{עזז}}$ and their usage. See No. 137.

g) רֵעִים substantive 0:7; cmp. 124) מרעים 10:6.

h) שִׁירָה 0:13; cmp. שִׁיר 11:61

i) α) קְצוֹת הָאָרֶץ 0:4; β) קָצֶה (הָ)אָרֶץ 3:14;[324] cmp.

33) קצוי ארץ 3:0.

C. j) דכא verb 4/3:14/15;[325] cmp. 6) דכה verb 5/6:0.

k) מלט Piel 5:22;[326] cmp. 105) פלט Piel 16/17:2.

D. 1) נגן verb 3:10;[327] cmp. 140) I זמר verb 39:0.

m) עתר verb 0:20; cmp. the synonyms הִתְפַּלֵּל, הִתְחַנֵּן

and 146) שִׁוַּע 13/12:9/10 which are all used in the psalms.
Further words with religious (cultic) meaning whose absence
from the psalms is striking are noted and discussed later.[328]

n) מַדּוּעַ 0(1):72;[329] cmp. לָמָּה 25+2 prose:149.

o) יָד of God 32+6 prose:122; cmp. 76) ימין of God
19:4 (זרוֹעַ of God is 11+3 prose:20).

p) "Power, might". α) אוֹן (outside the metaphor
רֵאשִׁית אוֹן, "first born son") 0:6; β) חָזְקָה/חִזְקָה*, חֵזֶק/חֹזֶק/חָזְקָה*
1:15;[330] γ) עֶצֶם, עָצְמָה, עֲצֻמוֹת 2:5;[331] δ) כֹּח 15+9 prose:101;
ε) גְּבוּרָה 18+4 prose:33.[332] Cmp. all these with 94) עז
43/42:(33?)34/35.

q) (עַל)(כִּסֵּא), "(sit/install) on (a chair/throne)"
1:50;[333] cmp. 17) (לכסא) 3:0.

III. THE PERVASIVENESS OF PSALM LANGUAGE

After this digression into the negative, let us return
to the positive. The 166 words, forms, and phrases which have
been presented here are the elements of the language of the
psalms which I was able to isolate. I do not pretend to have

exhausted the possibilities although I think I have come
fairly close to completeness in lexicography and morphology.
It is, as far as I am aware, the first attempt to describe
statistically the specific language of one part of the
literature of the Hebrew Bible. It is this statistical
method alone that enables the student of the Bible to speak
with assurance of psalm or wisdom or legal language and to
know whereof he is speaking. Already at this point it may
be apparent that, to a considerable extent, the language of
the psalms is not what the contents of the psalms might
suggest.

This investigation was conducted with no implicit
hypothesis as to possible results and, consequently, no
hypothesis as to nonlinguistic evaluations of those results.
Such evaluations will be made in the course of this study.
They are the theories and, as such, open for discussion.
The material, presented above, constitutes the data. The
main purpose of this study is to provide biblical research
with hitherto unknown facts.

In order properly to interpret these facts, one has to
consider more than the mere figure of 166 items. A statement
that psalm language is represented by these items would imply
that it is truly general in the psalms, that it permeates the
whole of the psalm literature. This is actually the case.
With very few and insignificant exceptions every psalm has its

share of it.[334] Furthermore, a sampling by pages of one
fourth of the psalter shows that items of psalm language
are found on every page with a frequency ranging from 9 to
31 items per page.[335] Of far greater importance, however,
is the fact that its elements are rather evenly spread over
all types of psalms. In order to show this, the psalms of
the Psalter are classified in accordance with Gunkel's
Gattungen.[336] The items 1-70, 72-84, i.e. the first half
of the preceding lists,[337] are allocated to their respective
Gattungen. Example: 7) רוממ ה occurs twice in lamentations of
an individual (22.3; 39.3), once in a psalm of confidence
(62.2), and once in a hymn (65.2).[338] The table on the
following page shows the result of the allocations.

It is col. IV which particularly attracts our attention.
It informs us of the distribution of psalm words within the
individual Gattungen. If we disregard those Gattungen which
are sparsely represented in the Psalter (col. I 3, 9, 14;
they occur [col. II] 2-5 times) and are, therefore, statistically unimportant, we find that, with two exceptions, the
average number of tested psalm words and forms in one psalm
ranges from 3.2 to 5. And the exceptions can only technically
be so called. One, I 12 (2.1 items per poem), is rather an
affirmation of the general finding: Since the "oracles",
being parts of whole psalms, are much shorter than the poems
of the other Gattungen, the number of items per "oracle" is
necessarily smaller. The other is I 7 (5.4 items per poem).

I Gattungen	II Number of Gattungen in the Psalter[339]	III Number of the first half of psalm words and forms in a Gattung	IV Average number of the first half of psalm words in a psalm of a Gattung (ratio of col. III to col. II)
1. Hymns	35	136	3.9
2. Songs of Zion	6	20	3.3
3. Songs of Jhwh's ascension to the throne	5	14	2.8
4. Lamentations of the people	16	70	4.4
5. Royal songs	10	50	5
6. Lamentations of individuals	50	160	3.2
7. Psalms of confidence	7	38	5.4
8. Thanksgiving songs of individuals	14	61	4.4
9. Thanksgiving songs of the people	2	4	2
10. Legends	3	13	4.3
11. Didactic psalms	1	3	3
12. Oracles and prophetic influence	8	17	2.1
13. Wisdom psalms	5	25	5
14. Liturgies	2	5	2.5

In establishing the psalms of confidence as an extra Gattung,
I ventured a little beyond Gunkel. Gunkel treats them as a
sub-Gattung within the Gattung of the lamentations of individuals out of which it emerged.[340] The present distinct contents of the psalms of confidence may justify the setting up
of a special Gattung, but in terms of Gattungsgeschichte which
emphasizes language and form they belong together. Taking,
then, both Gattungen (I 6 and 7) as one, the average number
of psalm words and forms in one psalm is 3.5. This adjusted
figure also narrows the limits slightly to 3.3-5 items per
poem. (But even admitting col. I 3 with its 5 psalms in the
Psalter, thus excluding merely those Gattungen which occur
no more than twice each, the adjusted limits would be extended
to 2.8-5 items per poem only.) This almost even distribution
of items of psalm language among the Gattungen, together with
the earlier observation of the remarkable frequency of items
on all sampled pages, justifies the statement that psalm
language is a basic and general feature of psalm literature
in all its parts.

The generality of psalm language can be made manifest
not only in figures, but also by the extent of its use and by
its "Sitz im Leben".[341] It is a matter of discussion whether
the authors of the psalms were pious individuals, i.e. free
poets, or members of Temple singer guilds whose profession it
was to provide psalms for worship.[342] The arguments of both
sides are based on internal evidence and general considerations

which are interpreted either way. There is, however, one
group of psalms or psalm-like poems whose author is known:
the so-called "Confessions" of Jeremiah.[343] Jeremiah is the
most distinctive personality of ancient Israel of whom we
know. His life and fate, though in broad lines similar to
those of some other prophets, are unique. His "Confessions"
bear clear witness to his fate. They are his own reflections
about it. Furthermore, wherever he speaks to us, we are
impressed by his own characteristic style. And yet, these
"Confessions", though no less Jeremianic in style than his
other utterances, are characteristic examples of psalm
language. The following words, exclusively or chiefly psalm
property, occur in the "Confessions": 19) מנוס (Jer 16.19);
27) עז (16.19); 47) אפסי ארץ (16.19); 73) מחסה (17.17);
87) I נצח (15.18); 102) עלז√ (15.17); 124) מרעים (20.13);
139) II הלל√ (17.14; 20.13); 147) שיר verb (20.13). Likewise,
their phraseology is in part known from the other psalms:
בֹּחֵן כְּלָיוֹת וָלֵב (11.20; similar 20.12 [but probably not original
here]; cf. No. 172); הַיְשֻׁלַּם תַּחַת טוֹבָה רָעָה (18.20; cf. Ps 35.12;
38.21; outside Gen 44.4); וּפַחִים טָמְנוּ לְרַגְלָי (Jer 18.22; cf.
Ps 140.6; 142.4); זָכְרֵנִי וּפָקְדֵנִי (Jer 15.15; cf. Ps 106.4);
כִּי שְׂמֵחָי; יֵבֹשׁוּ רֹדְפַי וְאַל אֵבֹשָׁה אָנִי (Jer 17.18; cf. Ps 31.18);
כִּי כָרוּ שׁוּחָה (Jer 20.10; cf. Ps 31.14); כָּבַת רַבִּים מָגוֹר מִסָּבִיב
(Jer 18.20); כִּי כָרוּ שִׁיחָה לְלָכְדֵנִי (18.22; cf. Ps 57.7; לְנַפְשִׁי
119.85); מַחְסִי אַתָּה בְּיוֹם רָעָה (Jer 17.17; cf. Ps 71.7; 91.9;
142.6); שְׂאֵתִי עָלֶיךָ חֶרְפָּה (Jer 15.15; cf. Ps 69.8 [89.51]).[344]

37

Psalm style imposes itself so strongly on Jeremiah's prayers
that, at times, he says things which are no longer in accord
with reality.[345] He praises God כִּי הִצִּיל אֶת נֶפֶשׁ אֶבְיוֹן מִיַּד
מְרֵעִים.[346] And yet, Jeremiah was neither poor,[347] nor for-
saken and politically isolated.[348] Or he supplicates רְפָאֵנִי
יהוה וְאֵרָפֵא[349] and laments לָמָּה הָיָה כְאֵבִי נֶצַח וּמַכָּתִי אֲנוּשָׁה מֵאֲנָה
הֵרָפֵא.[350] If these passages occurred in the Book of Psalms,
it would be taken for granted that the speaker were ill.[351]
Here it is likewise evident that Jeremiah does not pray for
recovery and that his words do not reflect any physical
condition. In ancient times nobody sought to be original.[352]
The shelter of convention, however awkward to modern readers,
was abandoned only in case of utmost need. In the oral com-
munication with God, psalm language and form were the shelter.
They covered great and small, the lonely genius and the man
in charge of the regular Temple service.[353]

CHAPTER III

HISTORICAL CONSIDERATIONS

I. THE AGE OF THE SPECIES OF THE ISRAELITE PSALMS

A. Content-Diction Relationship in the Biblical Psalms

The method of establishing psalm language is a statistical one. Since in science the method creates the object,
the only statements one can make about psalm language are
quantitative: A certain expression occurs so many times in
the psalms and so many times outside; a certain grammatical
form is predominantly psalmic.[354] So restrictive a formulation
of methods and results provokes the question: Can the language
of the psalms, established by the above method and listed in
its elements in the preceding chapter, also be described in
qualitative terms? Can a relationship be discovered between
the contents of the psalms and their diction? Being familiar
with the concepts of the psalms, would one a priori expect to
find what has in this study been called "psalm language" as
their adequate or natural expression? For many a word,
notably Nos. 138-147, but also others, this question is
unhesitatingly answered in the affirmative. But psalm
language as a whole calls for detailed investigation.

1. Cases Where Relationship Is Possible

Usually it is not possible to tell whether the predominant use of a certain word in the psalms is actually
prompted by its meaning. It may be in some cases, but not
in others. In the following, the linguistic material as
listed in Chapter II is grouped according to psalm concepts
wherever it lends itself to such grouping. It is borne
in mind that those elements of psalm language which correspond to psalm contents indicate the possibility but not the
actuality of a genuine and causal relationship between
psalm contents and psalm diction.

First a group of words for God and concepts associated
with Him.[355]

Names and epithets: 19) מנוס ; 22) סלע ; [23) סתר]
27) עז , "refuge"; 38) משגב ; 57) מגן ; 73) מחסה ; 74) ים ;
96) עליון ; 110) צור .

Splendor, theophany, honor, entourage, abode: 11) יפע
verb; 14) שסן/שמו כבוד ; 20) סביבותיו , סביביו ; 21) סך ;
60) הוד והדר ; 62) היכל קדשך/קדשו ; 81) מכון .

Holiness, righteousness, power: 35) רוח קדשך/קדשו ;
44) אמונה ; 71) חסד ; 76) ימין ; 79) מישרים ; 116) קדשו as
genitive; 165) active and passive...

Deeds, wonders: 30) עשה פלא ; 78) נוראות ; 80) כון
Polel..; 103) פלא ; 104) נפלאות ; 107) פעל פעלה ...of God.

Protection, salvation (and man's thanks for them),

retribution, punishment of the wicked: 25) עודד Poel, Hitpoel;
39) שחק verb...; 56) גמל verb; 68) חלץ II √; 69) חנן Qal;
72) חסה verb; 89) סתר Hiphil...; 105) פלם Piel; 119) בָּ(חַבִּים) ראה
+ enemy...; 121) רום Polel, Hiphil...; 122) רום verb + קרן;
126) שגב verb; 164) (ו)אני אמרתי.

Commandments: 26) עדות 31) פקודים ; 93) עדה.

The second group includes words for pious individuals
and related concepts. They are:

Righteous, faithful: 13) לב/רוח + נכון ; 15) ישרי לב ;
ואנחנו/ואני 163) ; חסיד 70)...

God fearing: 12) יראי יהוה/אלהים ; 77) יראיו.

Israel, the heritage of God: 86) נחלה.

Blessed: 49) אשרי־.

Hopeful, yearning: 75) יחל Piel; 117) קוה verb;
125)שבר√.

Joyous: 55) גיל verb.[356]

Words for evil, distress, destruction are noted in the
following.[357]

Evil: 29) עתק ; 123) רמיה.

Wicked: 4) רשעי ארץ ; 9) הוללים ; דוברי כזב/שקר(ים) ;
53) גאים ; 64) זדים ; 97) עלל I Poel...; 124) מרעים.

Foes: 41) שוררים ; 113) צר II ; 114) צורר ; 118) קמים
127) שטן verb; 132) שכנים.

Distress, oppression: 5) דך ; 28) עטה + shame; 112) צר I.

Desertion by God: 66) זנח Qal; 90) סתר Hiphil (Niphal)

41

פנים + of God.

Destruction: דחה (58 ; הוה II (61.

Netherworld: אפף√ (2 ; עבר (24 verb, with water as subject; משברים (40 ; מצולה (109 ; שחת (131.

Words for prayer, praise etc. certainly constitute a group by itself. They are listed as Nos. 138-147.[358]

The last group comprises words which denote long extended time, "eternity".

נצח I (87 ; עדי-עד (91 ; לעד (92 ; עולם (98 עולם, לעולם;
(ל)עולם ועד (99 ; מעתה ועד עולם ; עולמים (101 ...[359]

2. Cases Where Relationship Is Not Possible

The following items cannot generally be brought into relation to the religious, intellectual, or emotional experiences of the authors of the psalms:

אנף (1 Qal; נסר√ (3 ; דכה (6 verb; דומיה (7 ; הגיון (8;
זלעפה (10 ; כחש (16 Piel, "cringe"; (ל)כסא (17, "(sit...) on (a chair...)"; 18) לחם I Qal; צמת (32 Piel, Hiphil; קצוי (33
אלים (43 ; תך (42 (sing.); מרמות (36 (pl.); רגש (34 ; ארץ
אמר (45 (sing.); אמרה (46 ; אפסי ארץ (47 ; ארץ (48 as genitive...;
אשורים (50 ; בל (51 ; בני אדם (52 ; גאות (54 ; הגה I (59 Qal;
הלך (63 Piel; זכר (65 ; חיה (67 ratio Piel to Hiphil; מוט (82
verb; מלכי ארץ (83 ; נבע (84 Hiphil, "speak"; נדיבים (85 (pl.);
סבב (88 verb...; עז (94, "might; עטף II (95 Hitpael...;

102)√עלז ...; 106) פעל verb; 108) פעם, "foot"; 111) ציץ verb;
115) קדם verb; 120) רבת adverb; 128) שיח verb; 129) משגא;
130) II√שוה, "make"; 133) משכן pl....; 134) תבל ; 135) תהומות
pl.; 136)√שיש ...; 137) I√עזז ; 148-152) the grammatical
number of... musical instruments...; 153-162) various grammatical formations; 166) poetic parallelism...(a b c ∥ a b d...).

It is immediately evident that some of these items
cannot be associated with any definite content. These are
the grammatical formations (Nos. 153-162) which are used
instead of others, identical in function and similar in form.
Of the same kind are Nos. 148-152 and also those nine listed
and discussed in n. 359, as well as Nos. 17, 63 and the like.
Then there are vocables for general objects, such as Nos. 50,
108, that can certainly not be credited to the religion of
the psalms. But also words for more specific concepts,
among them Nos. 7, 82, 128, are found in such divergent
contexts and point to such contrary directions that it is
not possible to attribute their frequency to the importance
of any particular concept which they might symbolize. For
instance, No. 82 (מוט verb) quite often has as subject the
earth or the mountains (they do, do not "totter"), the psalmist
(he did [in the past], he will not [in the future]), or the
wicked. The number of these items which are part of psalm
language by statistics but altogether nonrelatable to psalm
contents is considerable: 64 out of 166 or 38.5 percent.
One may well doubt, therefore, whether all the words whose

usage one might have attributed to their relation to psalm
contents, actually owe their frequency in the psalms to their
meaning.

3. Seeming Relationship Proves Unreliable

It is true, great frequency of some expressions in
the psalms and concentration of others on definite psalm
concepts invite occasional speculation whether there is a
causal nexus between psalm thought and psalm language. The
following words lend themselves to such reflections. (They
are grouped according to concepts, following the order of
pp. 39-41.) First divine epithets that occur exclusively or
predominantly in the psalms: [סתר(23] ; סלע(22 ; מנוס(19
עז(27 ; משגב(38 ; מגן(57 ; מחסה (73) ; צור(110 . All are
variations of the theme of protection which finds further
expressions in 25) עודד Poel, Hitpoel; 56) גמל verb;
68) II √חלק; 69) חנן Qal; 72) חסה verb; 89) סתר Hiphil (Niphal)
...; 105)פלט Piel; 121) רום Polel...; 126)שגב verb. The
presence in the psalms of those words becomes remarkable
when compared with their absence or quantitative insignificance
outside. Were it not for the psalms, the concept of God as
the protector of man in need would not have been known to
have been prominent in ancient Israel. - In the minds of
biblical scholars, the idea of the holiness of God is generally
connected with certain parts of the legislative as well as
the prophetic literature. It is, however, the psalms which

44

less frequently than the rest of the Bible fail to add the
genitive קדשו (116) to anything which pertains to God;[360] which
use the expression היכל קדשך/קדשו (62) more often than all the
other parts of the Bible together, but never say הֵיכָל , הֵיכַל,
הֵיכַל יהוה , which are so frequent outside;[361] which appear
to be the soil where the concepts of the רוח הקדש and the
ἅγιον πνεῦμα have their roots (No. 35).[362] - It is in the
other parts of the Bible that "wonders" play their role.
And yet, how intensely must the thinking and the yearning of
the worshippers have been concentrated on miracles if the
three words נפלאות (104) ;פלא (103) ;נוראות (78)[363] are psalm
words. In this connection it is appropriate to note that
expressions for "hope", "yearn" are also elements of psalm
language: יחל (75) Piel; קוה (117) verb; שבר (125) . - Two synonyms for commandments or law are exclusively psalm property:
עדות (26) ; פקודים (31) , to which the psalm word עדת (93) may be
added. Does this permit us to meditate about the role of the
Torah in Temple circles? - Comparing the psalm expression
ישרי לב (13) with ישרים which is typical of Proverbs,[364] one
may be tempted to say that the common sense of the proverb
does not go beyond the visible and practical behavior of man,
whatever his motives may be, while the religion of the psalms
is characterized by what the Talmud says of prayer: הקב"ה
ליבא בעי , "God desires the heart".[365] Further in the lists
we find five psalm words for "evil doers": הוללים (9) ;
מרעים (124) ; זדים (64) ; גאים (53) ; רשעי ארץ (37) . So prevalent

is the subject of evil (fear, prayer for help and vengeance,
and the like) in the psalms that a special vocabulary, peculiar
to the psalms, has been developed for it. Of a similar kind are
psalm synonyms for "enemies": שוררים (41) ; צרII (113) ;
צורר (114) ; קמים (118) ; שכנים (132).

Nevertheless, one may doubt the significance of
establishing word-concept relations and expounding psalm
language for psalm thought. The following example shows
that here one cannot be certain even of what seems to be the
most obvious and soundest conclusion. The psalm word חסד (71)
is frequent both in psalms and outside. But what is noteworthy is the grammatical or logical <u>genitivus subjectivus</u>
in either part of biblical literature. In the psalms it is
chiefly God (96 times + 12 times prose), but hardly ever
man (2 times), while outside it is 27 times God and twice
as many (57 times) man. So overwhelming is the proportion
of these figures that it seems hard to avoid the conclusion
that in the religion of the psalms there is little room for
חסד of man. And yet, this reasoning cannot be right. A man
who has or practices חסד is a חסיד.[366] This word is not
only an item in our lists (No. 70), occurring 26 times in
the psalms, but also "virtually an exclusive psalm term."[367]
That means, the only part of the Bible which associates חסד
with man is the psalms. The two inferences from psalm language
to psalm contents, using the same method and applying it to
virtually identical material, produce diametrically opposite

results. The outcome of the inquiry into the relation between
psalm language and psalm concepts may be summarized as follows:
a) 38.5% of the elements of psalm language are absolutely not
relatable to psalm contents. The relatability of a considerable
part of the remaining 61.5% thus becomes questionable. b) Where
establishment of a causal relation seems most justified, one
arrives at an impasse.

B. Psalm Language and Semitic Dialects
Closely Related to Hebrew

Since psalm contents can be held accountable for psalm
diction only to some degree, it becomes imperative to look for
an additional cause for the peculiarities of the idiom of the
psalms. The one which first comes to mind is the tendency of
prayer in general to perpetuate, at a later time, the common
language, secular or sacred, of an earlier period. There is,
however, no direct way of demonstrating this principle in our
case. It ought to be shown that the psalms, themselves part
of the Bible, have preserved remnants of older stages of Hebrew
development. But these stages are not known to us. The oldest
Hebrew inscription, the Gezer Calendar, comes from biblical
times. The Cannanite glosses together with Canaanisms in the
Akkadian language of the El-Amarna letters may cautiously be
regarded as representing a precursor of classical Hebrew, but
they alone are too few to extend appreciable help.

The indirect way leads via the other Canaanite dialects

and Ugaritic with side glances at Northwest Semitic material,
incorporated in Old Babylonian texts. If one can find
linguistic features which are common to the biblical psalms
and Canaanite dialects but which are not at all or only to
a limited extent shared by the rest of the Bible, one may
safely infer that this is a common heritage from a time when
Hebrew and other branches of Canaanite were not yet separated.
The language of Hebrew devotional poetry, one would conclude,
has preserved remnants of an earlier linguistic stage which
has been lost or almost lost in common contemporary Hebrew.
It does not matter, of course, whether the Canaanite sources
from which the comparative material is culled are of an early
or a late date, since after separation, each linguistic branch,
developing in its own way, possibly retained features which
other branches had discarded.

With material from Ugarit, conditions are slightly
different. Any conclusions that may be drawn from it are
not based on the assumption that Ugaritic is genetically to
be classified as a Canaanite dialect.[368] Still, comparison
is legitimate. Stylistic similarities between Ugaritic and
biblical literature are too numerous and too detailed to
permit the exclusion of Ugaritic material from this investigation. Furthermore, in linguistics one cannot work with the fami-
ly tree theory alone, but has to allow that certain phenomena
are to be explained by the wave theory.[369] This holds true
particularly for specific linguistic activities such as the

language of the cult or of elaborate literary forms. In our
case we will be the more inclined to concede the possibility
of mutual linguistic influence the more we realize that,
during the greater part of the second millennium B.C.,
Canaanite and Ugaritic were similar enough to one another
for such influence not to cause too much divergence from the
peculiar norm of either language.[370]

1. Canaanite Material

Here, then, is the Canaanite material which I have
been able to collect for comparison with the language of the
psalms. The psalms-to-outside ratios are added to the elements
of psalm language. If the compared Canaanite material needs
no elaboration, reference is made to the glossaries of Har.,
pp. 71-156, or Sl., pp. 353-377,[371] and the number of
occurrences, listed in those glossaries, is added.

1) אגף Qal (5+2 prose:0) - Mesha Stone 5.

3) (נמר)√(5:0) - Sl. 198.2 אש נסר עשתרת, "to whom Astart
rendered good/ whom A. protected."[372]

25) עודד Poel...(3:0) - Zkr Inscription[373] 1.12
עודד?.[374]

27) עז , "refuge"(7[8?]:0[1?, 2?] and/or 94) עז , "might"
(43/42:[33?]34/35) - Sl. 95.1 and part of at least eight theophoric nomm. pr. [375]

43) אלים (4:1/2).[376]

51) כל (39:25) - very frequent, occasionally lengthened

אֵיבֶל, אָבַל.[377]

[63) הלך Piel (15/14/13:10/11/12) - Mesha 14 f.:וָאֵהֲלֹך (Qal?, Piel?).]

65) זכר (13:10) - Sl. 209; usually סכר for which there are four references.[378]

68) II√חלק (9:4) - Sl. 194.5 and part of at least six (theophoric) nomm. pr.[379]

69) חנן Qal with God as subject (26:14) - three (four) references of separate verbs[380] and very frequent as predicate in sentence names with a deity as subject.[381]

96) עליון divine name or epithet (20:6).[382]

98) לעולם, עולם (70+3 prose:65) - seven references.[383]

[105) פלם Piel, "save" (16/17:2).[384]]

106) פעל verb(27:26) - passim.[385]

[107) פעלה, פעל... of God (12[13]:6) - two nomm. pr.[386]

108) פעם, "foot" (8:4[5]) - two references.[387]

119) ב ראה + enemy (6:1) - Mesha 4.

155) מ‍ֹ suffixes used with substantives...(51:41) - three occurrences noted.[388]

157) הֵ‍ז, זּ‍, זּ‍ determinative pronouns...(18/17:6/7) - five(six) occurrences.[389]

164) a) אני אסרתי (4:0) - anāku aqabbi (EA 286.39).[390]

2. Ugaritic Material

The following list contains Ugaritic material for comparison.

17) (לבסא), "(sit...) on (a...throne)" (3:0) –
b‘l.ytb.lks[ỉ...] bn dgn.lkḥ[ṯ...391];392 ytb.lkḥṯ ȧl’yn b‘l.393

32) צמח Piel, Hiphil (11:0) – three references.394

43) אלים (4:1/2).395

48) ארץ as genitive...(14:14) – bn.nšm// hmlt.ȧrṣ,
"mankind// multitudes of the earth";396 ỉlm.wnšm// hmlt.ȧrṣ,
"gods and men// multitudes of the earth".397

51) בל (39:25) – at least four references.398

55) גיל verb (20/18:20/22) – one reference.399

59) I הגה Qal (12[13]/11:9/10[11]) – one reference.400

67) חיה ratio of Piel to Hiphil (in the psalms 11+n+1
prose:1; outside 31:21) – D-stem:401 ȧp ȧnk.ȧ̇hwy ȧqh[t], "so
shall I indeed revive Aqht";402 hẇt l.ȧ̇hw, "him I would have
kept alive".403 There is no Š-stem of this verb which would
correspond to the Heb. Hiphil.

80) כון Polel..., with God as...subject (13+1 prose:4) –
one reference.404

96) עליון divine name...(20:6) – Ugaritic in the form
‘ly:405 lȧrṣ m[ṭ]r.b‘l wlšd.mṭr.‘ly, "unto the earth Baal
rained and unto the field rained ‘ly".406

105) פלט Piel, "save" (16/17:2) – one reference.407

108) פעם "foot" (8:4[5]) – very frequent in Ugaritic
in the form p‘n.408

109) מצולה (8+1 prose:3) – one reference.409

113) II צר (30+1 prose:30/31) and 114) צורר (12:5) –
occurs as ṣrt(// ’b), two references.410

118) קמים, "enemies" (6:2) - one reference.[411]

120) רבת adverb (5:2) - rbt.ìlm.lḥkmt, "very wise hast thou shown thyself, O El".[412]

[133) מסכן pl. form with sing. meaning (5[4]:2) - probably one reference.[413]]

135) תהומות (pl.; 11:3) - Ugaritic seems to prefer the dual thmtm.[414] In Hebrew the pl. has replaced the dual here as it has so often. תהומות is, as it were, a slightly modernized archaism.

157) זה, זו, זו determinative pronouns...(18/17:6/7) - Ug. ḏ, very frequent.[415]

162) מאד before the modified word (3:0) - one/two references.[416]

165) Active and passive... of the same verb...(8:1) - [ḥ]š̌.bhtm.[bn]ḥš̌.rmm.hk[lm]ḥš̌.bhtm.tbn[ ]ḥš̌.trmmn.hk[lm], "quickly [build] a house, quickly erect a pal[ace], quickly let a house be built, quickly let a palace be erected."[417] åšsprk.ᶜm.bᶜl šnt.ᶜm bn ìl.tspr.yrḫm, "I shall cause thee to count years with Baal, Thou shalt count months with the god(s)."[418]

166) Poetic parallelism...a b c // a b d...(30[32?]/29[30]: 19[20?]/20[21?]).[419]

3. Northwest Semitic ("Amorite") Material

The following Northwest Semitic ("Amorite") words can be extracted from nomm. pr. which occur in Old Babylonian texts and compared with elements of psalm language.

23) סתר sensu religioso (7:0) - nomm. pr. sí-it-ri-AN sí-it-ri-e-lum,[420] ᵐsí-it-ri-ᵈadad,[421] "God/Adad is my protection".[422]

38) משׁגב sensu religioso (10:0) - n. pr. Sagbi-Adad, "Adad is my stronghold".[423]

70) חסיד (26:3) - n.pr. ḫa-sí-da-nu-um,[424] חסיד + hypocoristic ending -ān.[425]

110) צור divine epithet (18:9) - n. pr. Sūrā-Ḫammū, "Ḫammu is the rock/mountain".[426]

157) זָה, זּו, זּו determinative pronouns...(18/17:6/7) - n. pr. zu-(ú)-i-la, "He of the god".[427] [428]

The particular linguistic affiliation of the dialect represented in part by these words[429] cannot be decided with certainty. Hebrew seems to be the next of kin[430] with Aramaic a close second,[431] while Ugaritic is a possibility.[432] Yet it must be said that we can hardly expect a clear cut distinction between the later individual languages of the Northwest Semitic group as early as in Old Akkadian times. Nor should we forget that inscriptions and extant sacred literature have crystallized only a few visible points in the continuum of Semitic dialects that covered parts of the fertile crescent during the last two millennia B.C.[433] Therefore, this short comparative list of Northwest Semitic material, going back to the turn or the last third of the third millennium, is not out of place here.

4. Further Comparisons

It is here that we may profitably consider the list
of words which do not occur in the psalms.[434] We note some
interesting facts. The list includes three words or word
forms of otherwise common biblical use which are fully or
almost fully replaced by corresponding words and forms
typical of the psalms. They are:

a) אנף Hitpael [0:6; psalm language has 1) אנף Qal
5+2 prose:0].

k) מלט Piel [5:22; psalm language has 105) פלט Piel
16/17:2].

q) עַל (כסא), "(sit...) on (a chair...)" [1:50; psalm
language has 17) לְ(כסא) 3:0].

In regard to these words, Canaanite (in Nos. 1 [and
105]) and Ugaritic (in Nos. 17 and 105) go with the psalms,
thus isolating common, i.e. not psalmic, Hebrew.[435]

Hebrew has two sets of verbal stems which are
characterized by lengthening of the first root syllable.
In one set, morphologically corresponding to Arabic II (and V),
the syllable is closed, in the other, corresponding to
Arabic III (and VI), the vowel is lengthened. The first set,
the Piel, Pual, and Hitpael, is the commonly used set of the
Hebrew verb. The second set is very rarely used with the

strong Hebrew verb.[436] With the ע״ע and ע״ו verbs it is
still quite normal, though already on its retreat, giving
way to the first set.[437] I עלל occurs with the same meaning
in both sets. The first set, here entered as c) I עלל (0:6),
is not found in the psalms. The second set, 97) I עלל (5:2),
is psalm language. The psalms avoid the later development,
i.e. the first set with this class of verbs, retaining the
"good old" Poel.

Of the two Heb. words for "why", למה is formed in the
common Semitic way, "what for"; cf. Phen. לם, Aram. למא,
מה לום מה, אמא etc., Arab. لِمَاذَا, Akk. ana mīnim, ammīni.
n) מדוע is exclusively Hebrew, i.e. it is a Hebrew innovation;
a very old innovation, to be sure,[438] and a very common one,
to boot,[439] but nevertheless an innovation. Yet what had
been appropriate for a secular song in the twelfth or eleventh
century B.C., was not yet felt suitable for sacred poetry half
a millennium later.

Of the five words or word groups for p) "power, might",
lacking or rare in the psalms,[440] (two or) three are exclusively
Hebrew: α) און (0:6);[441] β) חזק...(1:15);[442] δ) פה (15+9
prose:101).[443] They also may safely be called Hebrew innovations.[444] How slowly did the psalms absorb those innovations
which were already centuries old in the days when most of them
were being composed? On the other hand, the only psalm word
of this meaning, 94) עז (43/42:[33?]34/35), is the one which

occurs as "might" or "mighty", in slightly different forms,
of course, in the relatively large number of Semitic languages:
Phenician, Ugaritic, Aramaic and South Arabic. One is tempted
to say: Psalm literature is the oldest literary species of
the Bible.

C. The Inception of Psalm Composition in Israel

But let us not anticipate. Turning back to the
comparison of actual psalm words, forms, and phrases with
Canaanite, Ugaritic, and "Amorite", we have found: 16/20[445]
items have been paired with corresponding words and forms
from Canaanite sources, 21/22[446] with analogues from Ugarit,
and 5 with pertinent words culled from the Old Babylonian
texts. Since 6 items (Nos. 43, 51, 96, 105, 108, 157),
belong both to the Canaanite and Ugaritic lists, one of them
(No. 157) figuring also in the "Amorite" list, and are, therefore, counted only once, the sum total is 35/40. This means:
Out of 166 elements of the language of the psalms, i.e.
elements which in classical Hebrew are known solely or over-
whelmingly from the psalms, 35/40 are known from closely
related languages of Israel's precursors or contemporaries.

If we are to appreciate these figures, we must bear
in mind several points. a) Psalm hapax and dis legomena as
well as relatively frequent, yet substandard words and forms
are not included in this study. Consequently, their Canaanite
and other parallels do not appear here.[447] b) Some elements

of psalm language are recognizable as such only by vowel signs
or vowel letters (e.g. Nos. 154 ff.). Our comparative material
very rarely indicates vowels in one way or another. c) No
Canaanite and, at best, only one Ugaritic prayer are known
to us.[448] It is true that the language of prayer draws from
earlier linguistic strata from all walks of life. But where
a particular devotional or cultic language from former ages
had already been in existence, large parts of it would certainly
have been incorporated in later prayers. For it is here that
linguistic tradition in meaningful. The religious content had
already been associated with linguistic form which was taken
over together with this content. One will remember that a
number of elements of the idiom of biblical psalms may possibly
be directly related to psalm contents. Our comparative material
which does not come from devotional texts necessarily contains
no parallels to these elements. d) The main factor quanti-
tatively restricting these extra-Israelite sources for comparison
is their paucity and, in the case of Canaanite, their monotony.
According to Albright,[449] the number of words, preserved in
the Ugaritic poetic texts, is little more than half the number
of the words of the Psalter. Only part of them could be
utilized here: Ugaritic epic style abounds in literal repetitions
which only duplicate or triplicate already known (parts of texts
with their) words. Also, the texts are often in such bad shape
that it is nearly impossible to do more with them than to
count their words. As to Phenician inscriptions, they belong

almost invariably to one of the two categories: dedications
and memorials, both next to uniform in content and expression.
Many of them are extremely short, differing from each other
only in the names of the persons mentioned. Lastly, the
"Amorite" sources consist only of nomm. pr. The usable
comparative material is thus reduced to a small fraction of
what it seems to be at the first glance. Under these circumstances, the number of 35/40 elements that can be bracketed
with corresponding words, forms, and phrases in those non-
Hebrew languages, i.e. 21.1%/24.1% of all the listed elements,
is astonishingly large.

Observations which were made concerning the negative
material (words and forms which are rare in, or absent from,
the psalms) point in the same direction: the idiom of the
Hebrew psalms is often better paralleled by the languages
of Israel's neighbors than by the idiom of the bulk of its
own literature, the Bible.

Our presumption has been confirmed. The comparison
with Canaanite and Ugaritic material, unfavorable as that
material is for this purpose, has shown that psalm language
has preserved parts of linguistic strata which are older than
biblical Hebrew in general. It is a safe conclusion that
many more elements of an earlier language could be demonstrated
as being embodied in psalm language were those Canaanite and
Ugaritic texts more suitable for comparison, not to mention the

possibilities were there prebiblical Hebrew material at hand.[449a]

A phenomenon, related in many respects to the language
of the biblical psalms, is the Akkadian so-called hymnic-epic
dialect. About twenty years ago, W. von Soden was able to
demonstrate in detail that certain Akkadian hymns and epics
from Old Babylonian times (ca. 1950-1550), all or most of
them from the later part of that period, show peculiarities
in grammar and vocabulary which link them over the centuries
with Old Akkadian (before ca. 1950 B.C.).[450] It does not
belittle von Soden's achievement nor disparage the difficulties
he had to overcome to say that in one respect his work was
easier than similar inquiries into the language and the
literature of ancient Israel: the history of the Akkadian
language, at least in its general outlines, is known as well
as its first stage, Old Akkadian. Thus the Assyriologist had
a frame of reference for his undertaking which the Hebraist
must reconstruct for his investigations, never hoping to have
more than a moderate success.[451]

Another, still closer parallel is the language of
Tannaitic prayer. Here one cannot point to a study comparable
to that of the Akkadian dialect,[452] as postbiblical Hebrew
has not been accorded adequate linguistic treatment. Yet even
a casual glance at those prayers reveals features which are
basic to classical Hebrew but are otherwise unknown to Middle
Hebrew. Some of these features are: The relative pronoun אשר,
the infinitive absolute, the infinitive construct with various

prepositions, the Waw conversive, and also the vocabulary.[453]
For the latter compare the following Mishnah: ...עַל פֵּרוֹת הָאִילָן
...אוֹמֵר בּוֹרֵא פְּרִי הָעֵץ...עַל פֵּרוֹת הָאָרֶץ אוֹמֵר בּוֹרֵא פְּרִי הָאֲדָמָה,
"...over the fruit of trees one says [the benediction: Blessed
art Thou...] who createst fruit of trees...over fruit of the
ground one says: Who createst fruit of the ground..."[454]
The Mishnah is composed in the vernacular of the second
century A.D. which has אִילָן for "tree", אָרֶץ for "ground",
and the pl. פֵּרוֹת for the collective "fruit"; but for prayers,
biblical words and forms are used instead: פְּרִי, אֲדָמָה, עֵץ.

The presence in the Bible of a particular devotional
language which has perpetuated otherwise obliterated or rare
forms of speech can be explained in two ways: 1) A genuine
Israelite idiom might have been partly preserved in it,
representing a stage of language history as old as, or older
than, the oldest pieces of the Bible.[455] 2) The language
of the biblical psalms is a continuation of the cultic
language used at the Canaanite shrines at the time of the
Israelite immigration into Palestine.[456] The Israelites
adopted it together with other customs, rites and beliefs.[457]
The two explanations are not mutually exclusive. Rather,
they indicate roughly the same age as the time to which we can
trace back the origin of psalm language, the time of the
immigration into Palestine of the Israelite tribes.[458] They
show that there was an uninterrupted tradition of psalm
idiom in Israel from its earliest times. And since this idiom

is bound to its corresponding literary form, the significant conclusion is reached: There was an uninterrupted tradition of psalm composition and psalm singing in Israel "since it became a nation." The psalms are not late comers in Israel's culture, nor was psalm composition in early times restricted to an occasional song here and there. Only a broad and steady stream of tradition could have carried so much of an early language into late poems.

The existence of a whole psalm literature at the time of Solomon has been proved by Albright. Albright was not the first to see that Ps 68 is not one poem but a catalogue of songs.[459] But he was able to assign it to this comparatively early age.[460] His dating, in turn, implies an earlier time for the rise of psalm singing at large in Israel. For where there is a catalogue, there is a number of items to be catalogued. In the case of Ps 68, it is hard to imagine that there was another reason for drawing up the catalogue than to single those thirty songs (according to Albright) out of a larger number of similar poems. We have, then, to allow some time for the growth and development of this type of poetry, and this will lead us back prior to the age of Solomon and probably prior to the age of David. Yet if the reasoning of the present study is correct, the time of the beginning of psalm composition in Israel has been projected more than two hundred years before the time of David.

II. THE END OF THE TIMES OF THE

BIBLICAL PSALMS

A. The Use of Key Items in the

Language of the Psalms and of Chronicles

In the preceding paragraphs an attempt has been made to utilize linguistic findings for dating the inception of devotional poetry in Israel. The psalms of the Bible have not been dealt with. About the time of their possible origin no more can be said than that it falls within the historic boundaries of the poetic species whose beginning has been dated above at the beginning of Israel's settlement in Palestine. For the establishment of the end of the period of the composition of the psalms, as far as they were accepted into the canon, a more direct approach, also linguistic, will be taken now: a comparison of the psalms with the Book of Chronicles. Certain cultic terms in the psalms will be isolated and collated with the corresponding terms as used in the Book of Chronicles. The Book of Chronicles is well suited for such a comparison. It abounds in cultic terms. There is full agreement among scholars as to the cultic conditions described in it. And while two distinct views are held in regard to the time of its origin, the difference between them does not exceed one and a half centuries, which is relatively small when compared with the differences in dating of many other biblical books. Actually we can by-pass existing differences of opinion and relate the linguistic material from Chronicles directly to a certain time and definite events.

In the presentation of the material, words for instruments of the Temple music, played in a chorus, are examined first. On pp. 23 f. it has been shown that the psalms use exclusively the form of the sing. for the collective (Nos. 148-152). The Book of Chronicles is equally consistent in the opposite use.

To psalms 148) כנור (eight [eleven] times in the psalms) Chron. כנורות corresponds (eight times in Chron. and once in Nehemiah).[461]

To psalms 149) נבל (four [six/seven] times in the psalms) Chron. נבלים corresponds (nine times in Chron. and once in Nehemiah).[462]

This law is also valid for the material of the following lists. They contain words for instruments used in the music of the Temple which are found in the psalms but not in Chronicles, and vice versa. Let us begin with the plus of the psalms over Chronicles.

150) עשור (three times in the psalms).

151) תף (three times in the psalms).

152) מחולה, מחול (four times in the psalms).

63

[שׁוֹפָר (four times in the psalms).463 The function
of the שׁוֹפָר in the psalms is apparently not the strictly
musical one of the accompaniment of the singing, but it plays
a role in particular pageants. In the book of Chronicles it
occurs once in a narrative telling of a covenant with God
which was concluded in the days of Asa.464]

The following instruments may conclude the list,
though they are of rare frequency:

עוּגָב (once in the psalms).465

צֶלְצְלִים (once in the psalms).466

מִנִּים (once in the psalms).467

The plus of Chronicles over the psalms is:

חֲצוֹצְרוֹת (ten times in Chron. and three times in Ezra-
Nehemiah).468

מְצִלְתַּיִם (thirteen times in Chron. and twice in Ezra-
Nehemiah).469

Also כְּלֵי שִׁיר 470 and its variant כְּלֵי דָוִיד 471 somehow
belong here. Yet no particular importance is attributed to
their absence from the psalms, as poetry tends to avoid such
general words as these which befit the lists and descriptions
of Chronicles.

Proceeding to the comparison of terms for other
cultic concepts, viz. praying, prayer and the like, the plus
of the psalms over Chronicles will again be taken up first.

140) I זמר verb (note the ratio 39:0!).

143) רום Polel, Polal, "praise" (9/10:0).[472]

146) IV√שוע (20/19:12/13; again the frequency in the
psalms is noteworthy).

Instead of a discussion of the plus of the Book of
Chronicles over the psalms, the linguistic usage of the time
of the Chronicler will be compared with that of the psalms.
There can be little doubt that the brief headings of most
chapters of the Psalter, disregarding pseudobiographical
remarks about the life of David,[473] are from the time of the
Chronicler or shortly thereafter. The Temple singer guilds
which are named in many headings, viz. בְּנֵי קֹרַח ,אָסָף,[474] [475]
and יְדוּתוּן,[476] flourished in that period. Later sources do
not mention them. In these headings we find the following
terms:

[140)] מִזְמוֹר. This word occurs 57 times in the
headings and only there. Nine times it is connected with
the name of Asaph,[477] seven times with the name of the Sons
of Korah,[478] and three(four) times with the name of Yeduthun.[479]
The word is unknown to the psalms proper, although the verb
I זמר is very frequently used there, and the substantives
זמיר and זמרה occasionally.[480]

מִכְתָּם. Meaning not known.[481] It occurs only in the
headings (six times[482]).

מְנַצֵּחַ, a musical term, variously explained as referring

65

to an instrument or a person.[483] Its occurrence is restricted
to the headings (55 times) and the frame of Hab 3.[484] Nine
times it is connected with the Sons of Korah,[485] four times
with Asaph,[486] and twice with Yeduthun.[487] [488]

מַשְׂכִּיל. No suggestion as to its meaning seems advisable.
It occurs thirteen times in the headings,[489] once in connection
with Asaph[490] and three times with the Sons of Korah.[491]
It also occurs in a marginal addition within a psalm.[492]

Two sets of words and forms for musical instruments
and for praying have been recognized. It is a case of clear-
cut dichotomy. With respect to the classes of literature,
words and forms are strictly characteristic; no lines are
crossed. Nor do the words and forms represent a negligible
quantity. They include on the psalm side 8 (12),[493] on the
Chronicles side 8 (9)[494] items, and for both sides the law,
peculiar to, yet different for each of them, of the use of
grammatical numbers for the collective of musical instruments.[495]
More remarkable is the fact that the 8 (12) items of the psalms
occur in 57 (58) poems. Quite often more than one item appears
in an individual psalm.[496]

But what lends importance to both sets is their being
technical-cultic. This precludes the possibility, already
unlikely because of the wide spread of the phenomenon, that
the words and the use of particular forms originated with the
whim of a few authors. Rather, they reflect different periods

in the history of the cult, and it is safe to assume that such a thoroughgoing change in cultic language is only concomitant with a more important change in religious outlook and practice.

Against this conclusion an objection may be raised. One might argue that the psalms, with their archaizing language, do not reflect contemporary linguistic usage and that, therefore, two distinct periods cannot be recognized from the two sets of terms. Specifically the Mishnah Berakhot 6.1, quoted on p. 59, might be referred to, which, rendering benedictions along with the instructions when to use them, exhibits two different kinds of vocabulary.

This argument is inconclusive. In the first place, attention is called to the fact that there are instruments, mentioned in the psalms but never in Chronicles, on which the devotees or, instead of them, Temple musicians are called upon to perform: 151) תֹּף , 152) מָחוֹל , מְחוֹלָה , and the rarely occurring צְלְצְלִים , עוּגָב , and מִנִּים . Naturally the inviter includes himself in the invitations; he is part of the crowd. These phrases, then, are the expressions of the psalmist's own intention, and though they are not formal vows, they are yet of a similar nature.[497] Now it is well known that in ancient days people were exceedingly careful with vows or utterances resembling a vow. Nobody would have voiced his intention in a holy place at a holy hour to perform something which he could not and would not do. It is, therefore, conclusive reasoning that those instruments, when mentioned in the psalms, were in actual use in the Temple music.

Further thought makes it evident that the linguistic circumstances in the Mishnah, referred to above, and the psalms are altogether incomparable, and that there is little likelihood that the language of the psalms is archaizing with regard to its cultic terms. In the Mishnah, a holy act, a prayer, is performed in a profane situation, a scene from daily life. No linguistic congruence between holy and profane is expected. In the psalms, the cultic terms refer to a situation which is itself cultic and which certainly has its adequate, i.e. cultic, language. It is highly improbable that there ever existed two widely different cultic idioms at the same time and in the same place; one which is attested to in the psalms, and the other which we know from Chronicles. Is it an even remotely sound assumption that the authors of the psalms, composed for prayer and performance in the Temple, anxiously circumvented the word מזמור if it was most common in the precincts of the Temple in their day? What prevented the writers of Chronicles in all their descriptions of praying and praising and playing from using the very frequent psalm verbs 140) I זמר; 143) רום Polel, Polal; 146) שוע, if not that, in their time, these verbs were dead, not only secularly but also cultically? We cannot escape the conclusion that the psalms in which these terms occur and Chronicles belong to different periods.

68

This conclusion has immediate validity for about
one third of the psalms, as this, it has been found above,[498]
is the number of poems in which the key items occur. But
its significance reaches far beyond. Only cultic terms,
by virtue of their exact meanings and use, are admissible
for collating the two groups of literature. The number of
cultic terms is rather limited. They belong to one or two
areas of meaning not touched upon by many individual poems.
Thus, the 1/3 proportion is a higher fraction than the
student might hope to find, and it entitles him to transfer
the inferences he has drawn from it to the bulk of the
remaining psalms. He is even more justified in doing so
if he admits the argumentum ex silentio of the cultic terms
peculiar to Chronicles, viz. that they are absent from psalm
literature, notwithstanding that many a psalm offers ample
semantic opportunity for their application. It is, therefore,
sound reasoning to amplify the above statement and say that
the psalms in general on the one hand, and Chronicles on the
other hand, belong to different periods. It belongs to the
nature of this reasoning to allow for some single psalms to
be dated in the time of Chronicles, but their number will not
exceed the very minimum.

B. Terminus Ante of the Biblical Psalms

It goes without saying that the period represented by
the psalms is the earlier of the two. Can we set its later

absolute limit? For a moment it seems that a <u>terminus ante</u>
can easily be established. Some of the forms characteristic
of Chronicles, viz.‏כנורות‏, נבלים, חצוצרות, מצלתים, שיר דוד כלי‏,
appear in the framework of the Memoirs of Nehemiah.[499] Since
the Memoirs are datable, having been written shortly after
433 B.C., the new linguistic period would begin not later than
about 430 B.C. But the passages containing these keywords
are generally regarded as Chronistic insertions and are,
therefore, not usable for our purpose.

In order, then, to find the absolute, though only
approximate <u>terminus ante</u> of the period represented by the
linguistic peculiarities of the psalms, one naturally turns
to the date of Chronicles itself. No full agreement has
been reached in this respect, but the picture is gradually
clearing up. Until World War I, scholars, with only few
exceptions,[500] did not date it before Hellenistic times,
preferring the first half or the middle of the third century
B.C. But Pfeiffer, who wrote as late as 1941: "It is generally
recognized that the Chronicler wrote between 350 and 250 B.C.,
or more exactly in the second half of this period,"[501] was
hardly presenting the prevailing opinion of his own day.
The following survey which does not claim to be exhaustive
certainly reflects the trend in this field since the end of
the first World War.[502] According to the following scholars
the Chronicler flourished about 400 B.C. or shortly thereafter:
W.F. Albright,[503] W. Rudolph,[504] J. Hänel,[505] G. von Rad,[506]

J. Hempel (less exact),[507] E. Sellin,[508] W.O.E. Oesterley,[509]
J. Meinhold,[510] J. Begrich (hesitating),[511] W. Möller,[512]
O. Eissfeldt,[513] M.Noth.[514] A.C.Welch who, like von Rad and
others,[515] holds that two persons are responsible for the
bulk of Chronicles, dates both back to the sixth century.[516]
The late daters include: F.X. Kugler,[517] G. Hölscher,
J.W. Rothstein,[518] R. Kittel,[519] W.O.E. Oesterley - T.H. Robin-
son.[520] After Pfeiffer's Introduction had appeared,
H.S. Gehman,[521] M.S. Segal,[522] and Th.C.Vriezen[523] sided
with the early daters; M. Noth who had changed his mind,[524]
A. Lods,[525] and H.S. - J.L. Miller[526] joined the late daters.

This writer, convinced like the majority of contemporary students by the arguments of Albright and his followers,
could acquiesce in accepting circa 400 B.C. or shortly thereafter as the date of the Chronicler. At this time, then,
the new set of cultic words and word forms was already in
use. This, in turn, means that, granting possible single
exceptions, the biblical psalms are of no later origin than
the fifth century B.C. - However, Albright's case, convincing as it is, rests on internal evidence and is provable
only within the limits of this kind of evidence. In general,
it is also desirable to separate the dating of the psalms from
the dating of any other piece of biblical literature.

This seems feasible. In fact, the _terminus ante_ of
the psalms on the whole is probably to be moved somewhat

before 400 B.C. It has been said above[527] that the change
of the cultic language is nothing but a function of comparable
changes in cultic ideas and practices. When, between the
fifth and the third centuries B.C.,[528] did such changes
take place? We have no report of that. We are altogether
poorly informed about many facets of the cult of the Jerusalem
Temple. Apart from ordinances concerning sacrifices and
single rites, the Bible contains no laws and rulings about
the course of the Temple service, its music and its pagentry.
So startling is the gap in legislation that Kittel thinks
that there did exist such written regulations which, for
some unknown reason, were not incorporated in the canon.[529]
Thus the historian has no fixed point against which he can
observe the development of this sector of the cult.

Under the circumstances, it is sound to combine the
required changes of the service with similar major changes
that happened during the period under consideration. The
events which offer themselves as those shifts are the religious
reforms inaugurated in the time of Ezra and Nehemiah.[530]
To be sure, the sources of that time do not disclose any
changes of the Temple service. Yet two details immediately
pertain here: 1) Both Ezra and Nehemiah took a keen interest
in the Temple;[531] 2) their memoirs have not come to us
complete.[532] Bearing these points in mind, nothing prevents
us from assuming that a report of a reform of the Temple
service was lost along with other portions of either of these

documents. Nor would we be at a loss to associate these
changes with certain known activities of Nehemiah. Radical
shifts of personnel, like those mentioned in Ne 13.7-9,
10-14, 30b-31a and particularly 13.28-30a, are opportune
moments to introduce new philosophies and practices. On the
other hand, one may argue that Nehemiah, as a nonpriest, did
not consider himself competent to reform or regulate the
service proper; the changes, rather, were instituted by
priests in the train of his (or Ezra's) overall reforms.
Be this as it may, Judaism underwent one of its most thorough
reforms in the later part of the fifth century B.C., and the
historian is certainly justified if he relates to them hitherto
undetected or unrelated phenomena likewise of a reformatory
nature. For our problem, this means that the time of Ezra and
Nehemiah, or shortly thereafter, is the required terminus ante
of the psalms.

At this point the study is ended. The present state
of our knowledge of the history of the Hebrew language
during the first half of the first millennium B.C. sets
rather narrow limits to a linguistic-historical inquiry into
the biblical psalms. The author feels that those limits are
not far beyond the field explored in the present study.

NOTES

1   Detailed studies are H. Holzinger, Einleitung
in den Hexateuch, 1893, pp. 93-110, 181-191, 283-291, 339-350,
411 f., 418 f.; J.E. Carpenter-G. Harford, The Composition
of the Hexateuch, 1902, pp. 381-425; J. Kräutlein, Die sprach-
lichen Verschiedenheiten in den Hexateuchquellen, 1908.

2   The latest study in this field is M. Pope, JBL
71(1952), pp. 235-243, where previous literature is mentioned
in the notes, pp. 235 f.

3   C.C. Torrey, The Composition and Historical Value
of Ezra-Nehemiah (BZAW 2), 1896, pp. 16-20; A.S. Kapelrud,
The Question of Authorship in the Ezra-Narrative, a Lexical
Investigation, 1944.

4   The justification for introducing this term will
become apparent in the course of this study.

5   The words "literature" and "literary" are used here
purely for the sake of convenience. They do not denote any
hypothesis concerning the time at which the psalms were committed
to writing. An early recording of the psalms is not very likely.
Note that among the many types of texts which have come to light
at the excavation of Ras Shamra at best one single short prayer,
UH, text 107, has been found (cf. O. Eissfeldt, El im ugariti-
schen Pantheon, 1951, p.61, n.). Nevertheless, it is beyond
doubt that the people of Ugarit sang and prayed (see UH 52:1 ff.,
23 f., 12; reference may also be made to UH 77:1, 37 f., 40,
45 f.).

6   Previous not particularly successful attempts of

classification of the psalms are mentioned in GuBe, pp. 8 ff.

7   Typical questions are: "Is a certain passage an eschatological one or is it not?" "Do we find 'wisdom' in the prophets, in the psalms, and, if so, where?" - The incommensurability in idiom and style of Proverbs and Job is one reason to question the advisability of classifying both under the common heading of wisdom literature.

8   This is meant in the broader sense which includes the mentioning of God in the third person as well as in the second. The difference between "He" and "Thou" psalms is merely a stylistic one; cf. GuBe, pp. 47 f., 122 f.

9   In 1 Ch 25.4b$^\beta$ a few lines in psalm style are concealed. No use is made of them for the study of psalm language. They are certainly an artificial concoction to provide names for the required number of 24 lots; cf. vv. 8 ff. Nor can the text be reconstructed with certainty; cf. the attempts in BH on the one hand, and of N.H. Torczyner, JBL 68 (1949), pp. 246 ff., on the other hand.

10   Cf. below, pp. 36 f.

11   E.g. Job 5.9-16; 9.4-13; 11.10 f. etc. Complete lists GuBe pp. 32 f.; E.G. Kraeling, The Book of the Ways of God, 1939, pp. 259 ff. (only for Job).

12   Even those passages of the Cairo Ecclesiasticus whose basic authenticity can be assured with reasonable certainty play no role in this study. To the extent that can be judged from Rabbinic quotations, the Cairo mss. and the versions,

the book abounds in artificial archaisms and biblical cita-
tions and cannot be regarded as a link in a living linguistic
tradition.

13   Statistics in philology is tedious for both
writer and reader, but, in certain cases, it is indispensable.
A. Sperber and K. Schlesinger have bared embarrassing mis-
statements that Hebrew linguistics has produced through
negligence of statistics or comparable methods. The former
has disproved the alleged rarity of the assimilation of
the נ of the preposition מן to the article: מה (JBL 62 [1943],
pp. 140-143); the latter the supposed normalcy of the word
order predicate-subject in the verbal clause. (The opposite
is true, VT 3 [1953], pp. 381-390. Only recently, in VT 2
[1952], p. 376, L. Köhler said that there were thousands of
examples for the word order predicate-subject in the simple
affirmative clause, but failed to quote one or to ask as to
the frequency of the inverse order.)

14   Throughout this study the term "outside" denotes
the Bible to the exclusion of the psalms.

15   For the same reason, words and forms that occur
in one poem only are not regarded as elements of psalm language,
but are entered, as Nos. 167, 186, 194 (206, 213, 218), into
the appended list of substandard words and forms (cf. p. 26).
However, occurrence in two poems only (Nos. 5, 18, 35, 153),
though somewhat limiting the significance of such words or
forms for the description of psalm language, is no reason for

their exclusion from the main lists. - Attention may be drawn
here to two other cases, discussed in nn. 62 and 141, on whose
inclusion in, and/or exclusion from, the lists, respectively,
one might prefer a different decision.

16   Nos. 168-170, 203 (209); see nn. 269 f., 272,
305.

17   Cf. M. Pope's criticism (l.c. [n.2], pp. 239 f.)
of methods and results of L. Köhler, Deuterojesaja...stil-
kritisch untersucht (BZAW 37), 1923, especially K. 3, 4, 5,
6-15, 36-44, 45, 46, 47, 50-53, 54-65; and similarly his
criticism (p. 237) of A.T. Olmstead's procedure.

18   Where in the notes only one of the two figures
is discussed, e.g. n. 44, this figure alone is given and is
preceded or followed by the colon. Thus "9:-" means:
"The 9 psalm occurrences"; "-:5" means: "The 5 outside occurrences". The figure which indicates the psalm occurrences
is sometimes followed by another figure. The explanation
of this will be given on pp. 9 f.

19   Nos. 67, 88, 148-152, 159, 163; in part Nos. 136 f.

20   E.g. Ps 18 and 2 Sam 22; Ps 118.14 and Ex 15.2
and Isa 12.2. The references are usually from the Book of
Psalms. With very short identical passages or splinters of
passages in different contexts, e.g. 93.1 and 96.10, all
occurrences are counted.

21   E.g. כִּי לְעוֹלָם חסדו.

22   E.g. 42.6, 12; 43.5.

23   E.g. 118.10b, 11b, 12b.

24   E.g. Hab 1.5 or infin. absol. with finite verb.

25   E.g. No. 31 with n. 63.

26   The corresponding invocation of v.35,which is poetry,suggests that v.36 may be poetry,too. V.35 has not been included in the psalm listed above, as it recurs, slightly adapted, in Ps 68.2.

27   The psalms are 8.5% of the whole Bible (repetitions and parallels as well as prose prayers are not counted). Disregarding lists of people, places etc. which do not yield usable material for the present study, the percentage of the psalms rises slightly to 8.8%.

28   On the other hand, compensating for the excluded prose material by making standards more severe, e.g. not counting words with a ratio below 6:0, might tend to exclude words and forms which are indeed characteristic of the psalms.

29   This is nothing but a restatement of the nonapplication of a factor as high as 12 which was discussed and decided above.

30   See n. 255.

31   Thus, three items, viz. Nos. 43, 53, 64, have been added on the basis of what appear to be small and cautious emendations.

32   2.12; 60.3; 79.5; 85.6; Isa 12.1. Prose 1 Ki 8.46; Ezra 9.14.

33   18.5; 40.13; 116.3; Jonah 2.6.

34   More accurately 3:0 (7.10; 12.2; 77.9) and 2:0
(57.3; 138.8), as two different roots are assumed: I גמר ,
"come/bring to an end;" II גמר , "render good", or, more
specifically, "protect." The dictionaries do not separate
them, but a semantic derivation of II from I is forced.
It seems preferable to consider II גמר related to גמל .
For II גמר cf. 1) the n. pr. גְּמַרְיָהוּ ; 2) the Phenician
phrase אש גמר עשתרת (see p. 48); 3) the second line of the
following couplet from the Akkadian epic of Etana: ^{11}ik-tám-
ra (!) maš-šak-ki-ia ^{GEME}ša'ilāti (e n - m e - l i)^{MEŠ}
^{12}az-li-ia i-na (var. ina) ṭu-ub-bu-ḫi ilāni^{MEŠ} ig-dam-ra
(var. -ru), "The priestesses have offered my libations in
abundance, they have rendered good to the gods by the slaughter
of my lambs" (S.Langdon, The Legend of Etana and the Eagle,
1932, Pl. VI, 11 f. = Pl. III 37 f. - kamāru occurs in the
G/Gt-stem with the meaning "to heap up, make abundant" in
Textes cunéiformes, Musée du Louvre III, lines 101, 257, 367
etc., and frequently in mathematical texts with the derived
meaning "to add", cf. O. Neugebauer - A.Sachs, Mathem. Cuneiform
Texts [Am. Or. Ser. 29], 1945, p. 167; F. Thureau - Dangin,
Textes mathém. babyl., p. 218 [I owe these references to
the kindness of Prof. I.J. Gelb of The Oriental Institute,
Chicago]. But even if one were reluctant to accept the reading
-tám- in the first word and preferred to read and translate
ig-dam-ra, "have completed/carried out" instead, one need not
join the common opinion, taking the second igdamra(u) as a mere

repetition of the first one. The two words are not identical
but form a pun, whatever the reading of the first one.
[For the pun as a stylistic device of the Akkadian epic cf.
simply E.A. Speiser in Ancient Near Eastern Texts..., ed.
J.B. Pritchard, 1950, p. 62, nn. 34 f., p. 93, n. 190, p. 94,
n. 202, and also the theological play on many of Marduk's
fifty names, Enuma Elish VI 123 ff.]).

35   5.7; 58.4; 63.12; 101.7.

36   9.10; 10.18; 74.21. Prov 26.28 is not clear;
not counted.

37   Qal 1:0 (10.10, or to be read as Niphal); Niphal
2:0 (38.9; 51.19); Piel 2/3:0 (44.20; 51.10 [89.11 ms.]).

38   22.3; 39.3; 62.2; 65.2. Cf. No. 179.

39   19.15; 92.4; Lam 3.62. (הַגִּון וַיְגִון פֶלָה is not counted;
cf. n. 492.) For the various meanings of the root see n. 93.

40   5.6; 73.3; 75.5 (מְהוֹלְלָי [102.9] may be added).

41   11.6; 119.53; Lam 5.10.

42   50.2; 80.2; 94.1; Dt 33.2; Job 10.3. - The two
outside occurrences of the verb which are transitive or have
another subject would bring the ratio up to 5:2. (Job 10.22
is by-form of IIעוף or I עיף; not counted.)

43   22.26; 25.14; 33.18; 34.8, 10; 85.10; 103.11, 13,
17; 111.5; 145.19; 147.11. Cf. No. 77. - יְרֵאֶיךָ 4:0 (31.20;
60.6; 119.74, 79) need not concern us, since the possessive
suffix of the second person is only natural in a literary
species which consists of addresses to God.

44   7.11; 11.2; 32.11; 36.11; 64.11; 94.15; 97.11.
The ratio in the parentheses includes יְשָׁרִים בִּלְבוֹתָם (125.4)
on the one hand, and יִשְׁרֵי לֵבָב (2 Ch 29.34) on the other hand.
יְשָׁרִים alone is a characteristic Proverbs expression: Prov fif-
teen times; Ps eight times (among which the above mentioned
125.4 is included [33.1; 49.15; 107.42; 111.1; 112.2, 4;
125.4; 140.14]); the rest of the Bible three times. Among
8(9):- times יִשְׁרֵי לֵב, not one is from a wisdom psalm, while
among the 8:-:- times יְשָׁרִים, three (49.15; 112.2, 4) are!

45   With שְׁמוֹ 29.2; 66.2. With שְׁמָךְ 79.9 (96.8=29.2;
not counted.)

46   With לֵב 57.8 (<u>bis</u>); 78.37; 112.7. With רוּח 51.12.

47   18.45 (2 Sam 22.45 has the <u>Hitpael</u>); 66.3; 81.16.

48   9.5; 132.11 f. The singular expression יָשְׁבוּ כִסְאוֹת
לְמִשְׁפָּט (122.5), though syntactically different, may have been
influenced by this characteristic psalm construction. -
הַיּוֹשֵׁב אֶל כִּסֵּא (Jer 29.16) occurs in a text which elsewhere,
too, confuses אֶל and עַל; cf. 27.19.

49   31.1 (<u>bis</u>); 56.2 f. לְחֻמֵי (Dt 32.24) is either
passive in form but active in meaning just as the <u>Niphal</u> of
this verb or a <u>nomen agentis</u> לֹחֵם(= יִלְחוֹם); cf. יְקוֹשׁ/יָקוּשׁ,
but also GK § 27n.

50   59.17; 2 Sam 22.3; Jer 16.19.

51   18.12 (metereological phenomena); 50.3 (metereol.
phenom.); 76.12 (man); 89.8 (angels), 9 (אֱמוּנָה as hypostasis);
97.2 (metereol. phenom.). Man and angels are God's סְבִיבוֹת,

just as they are his צְבָאוֹת, a term which means either group.
Metereological phenomena are regarded as angels (104.4; cmp.
148.2 f.).

  52   27.5; 42.5; 76.3. סָךְ (42.5) is pausal form
(GuPs, p. 181). Lam 2.6 שֻׂכּוֹ does not belong here; it probably
means "fence".

  53   18.3; 31.4; 42.10.

  54   27.5; 31.21; 32.7; 61.5; 81.8; 91.1; 119.114.
Cf. No. 89.

  55   42.8; 88.17 (where הֲמוֹנֶיךָ varies the theme of
"water;" cf. the next verse and also vv. 7 f.); 124.4 f.
The inclusion of a variant with another verb, viz.צָפוּ
(מַיִם עַל רֹאשִׁי) (Lam 3.54) would bring the ratio up to 5:0.

  56   Poel 146.9; 147.6. Hitpoel 20.9.

  57   Not·in the technical meaning of the tablets of
the Law.

  58   19.8; 78.5; 81.6; 119.88; 122.4. Cf. No. 93.

  59   28.7(8?); 46.2; 59.17, 18; 62.8; 81.2; Jer 16.19.
Possible outside occurrences Ju 9.51; Isa 49.5; cf. n. 137. -
It is not easy to come to a decision on this word and its
demarcation from its homograph "might" (√עזז). LVT, p. 693,
has more occurrences than are listed here; GB, pp. 575 f.,
has none. Both are inconsistent. LVT derives מָעוֹז from√עזז,
but renders it, inter alia, by "Zufluchtsstätte", p. 545,
while GB derives part of the מָעוֹז occurrences from√עזז,
p. 443.

60   71.13; 89.46; 109.29.

61   31.19; 75.6; 94.4; 1 Sam 2.3. This word is always found in connection with, or in the vicinity of, II√דבר, "speak".

62   77.15; 78.12; 88.11; Ex 15.11; Isa 25.1. This phrase is entered here by reason of the exclusiveness of its ratio. It is, however, rather a special case of No. 103.

63   19.9; 103.18; 111.7. In addition, this word is found 21 times in Ps 119.

64   Piel 88.17; 119.139. Hiphil 18.41; 54.7; 69.5; 73.27; 94.23 (bis); 101.5, 8; 143.12. (Qal and Niphal 0:3. Together 11:3.)

65   48.11; 65.6; Isa 26.15. Note further קְצָוֹת (יֹשְׁבֵי, 65.9) which would bring the ratio to 4:0.

66   verb 2.1. Nouns a) רֶגֶשׁ 55.15; b) רִגְשָׁה 64.3.

67   51.13; Isa 63.10 f.

68   10.7; 35.20; 38.13.

69   75.9; 101.8; 119.119. (רִשְׁעֵי הָאָרֶץ occurs once outside [Ez 7.21]. רְשָׁעִים is frequent in many parts of the Bible.) Cf. No. 48.

70   9.10 (bis); 18.3; 46.8; 48.4; 59.10, 17; 62.3; 94.22; 144.2. Profane meaning 0:2. Together 10:2. Cf. No. 126.

71   2.4; 37.13; 59.9.

72   42.8; 88.8; 93.4; 2 Sam 22.5.

73   5.9; 27.11; 54.7; 56.3; 59.11. - שׁוּרָי (92.12), a variant, may be added, bringing the ratio to 6:0.

74   10.7; 55.12; 72.14. The pl. occurs once
(Prov 29.13). By emendation one may add Ps 90.11 (וּמִי יָרֵא חֹרְךָ ;
עֶבְרָתֶךָ ; cf. BH) and Jer 9.4 f. (הֶעֱוּוּ נִלְאוּ שֶׁבְאָ:חֹךָ בְּחוֹךְ מִרְמָה ;
בְּמִרְמָה ; cf. BH), thus changing the ratio to 4:1

75   Also the following items occur in the psalms
only: 140) a) I זמר verb; 143) רום Polel..., "praise;"
150) עשׂוּר ; 153) נִי__ ...suffix...used with prepositions;
[160) חטה אֹזֶןךָ] 162) מאֹר preceding the modified word. They
have been grouped, however, according to principles which
determine subsequent lists, in order to bring different facets
of psalm language into sharper relief.

76   For details see above, p. 7.

77   29.1; 89.7; Ex 15.11; '58.2'. Outside Dan 11.36
(Job 41.17?). For the meaning see the end of n. 376.

78   33.4; 36.6; 40.11; 88.12; 89.2, 3, 6, 9, 25, 34,
50; 92.3; 96.13; 98.3; 100.5; 119.75, 90, 138; 143.1; Dt 32.4;
Isa 26.2; Lam 3.23. Ps 119.30 probably belongs here. On the
other hand, אמוּנה of man is distributed 1/2:21 (37.3, possibly
119.30; outside Ex 17.12 and the pl. Prov 28.20 not counted);
cmp. No. 71. Out of -:21 occurrences, more than 6 באמוּנה in
Kings and Chronicles mean "honestly", referring to the adminis-
tration of Temple property.

79   19.3 f.; 68.12; 77.9. אָמְרוּ (Job 20.29) belongs
here somehow, though going back to* אָמָר .- מִמָּלוֹת אֹמֶר (Hab 3.9)
has nothing to do with our word; cf. U. Cassuto, Annuario di
Studi Ebraici 2 (1938), p. 18. - Cf. No. 46.

80   12.7 (<u>bis</u>); 17.6; 18.31; 105.19; 147.15 (138.2; text?). In addition, this word is found nineteen times in Ps 119. Prov 30.5 is not counted; it is a psalm quotation (cf. Ps 18.31). - Cf. No. 45.

81   2.8; 22.28; 59.14; 67.8; 72.8; 98.3; 1 Sam 2.10; Jer 16.19.

82   רִשְׁעֵי אֶרֶץ 3:0 (see n. 69); 'א נְאֻמְנֵי 1:0 (10.18); מְגִנֵּי 'א 1:0 (47.10); 'א רִגְעֵי 1:0 (35.20); 'א מַלְכֵי 5:2 (see n. 124); 'א שֹׁפְטֵי 2:2 (2.10; 148.11); 'א עֲנִיֵּי 1:3 (76.10; of these four occurrences, three are Qeres for the Ketivs עֲנוּיֵי [76.10; Am 8.4; Zeph 2.3]); 'א זִקְנֵי 0:1; 'א אֲסִירֵי 0:1; נִכְבַּדֵּי 'א 0:2. The following genitive constructions do not belong here: דַּשְׁנֵי 'א (22.30; preferably יְשֵׁנֵי'); עַתּוּדֵי 'א (Isa 14.9); קְטֻנֵּי 'א (Prov 30.24). In the first two cases, ארץ means "netherworld" as in Jonah 2.7 and quite commonly in Akkadian. (For Ps 22.30, the meaning "soil" is possible, too.) The third case is from a proverb about small ground animals; ארץ indicates the element as in חַיְתוֹ 'א (Ps 79.2; Gen 1.24) as distinct from water and air.

83   1.1; 2.12; 32.1 f.; 33.12; 34.9; 40.5; 41.2; 65.5; 84.5 f., 13; 89.16; 94.12; 106.3; 112.1; 119.1 f.; 127.5; 128.1; 137.8 f.; 144.15 (<u>bis</u>); 146.5.

84   17.5; 37.31; 40.3; 44.19; 73.2. The text of 17.11 (which has אֲשֻׁרִים like Job 31.7) is not certain.

85   10.4, 6, 11, 15, 18; 16.2, 4 (<u>bis</u>), 8; 17.3 (<u>bis</u>),5;

21.3, 8, 12; 30.7; 32.9; 46.6; 49.13; 58.9; 78.44; 93.1;
104.5, 9 (**bis**); 119.121; 140.11 f.; 141.4; 147.20; Isa 26.10 f.,
14 (**bis**), 18 (**bis**); 33.20 (**ter**). Of the 39:- times, 6 are from
Isa 26 and 3 from Isa 33. The Qere in Hos 9.16 is not counted,
the Ketiv being preferable. For the odd concentration of the
word in certain books of the Bible see LVT, p. 128.

      86   11.4; 12.2; 14.2; 21.11; 31.20; 36.8; 49.3;
57.5; 58.2; 62.10; 66.5; 89.48; 90.3; 107.8; 115.16. Prose
Jer 32.19.

      87   94.2; 140.6 and the following nine emendations of
MT נּדֹים, most of them according to B. Duhm, Die Psalmen, 1899,
a.l., and H.L. Ginsberg, HUCA 23 I (1950-51), pp. 98 f.: 9.6,
16, 18, 20 f.; 10.16; 59.6, 9; 118.10. (Six are from one poem!
[Ps 9 f.]). The assumed error in MT goes back to the phonetic
variant *נֹאים=*נֹיים; the latter was then read נּדֹים. For a
similar error cf. No. 64.

      88   17.10; 89.10; 93.1; Isa 12.5; 26.10.

      89   9.15; 13.5 f.; 14.7; 16.9; 21.2; 31.8; 32.11;
35.9; 48.12; 51.10; 89.17; 96.11; 97.1, 8; 118.24; 149.2;
Isa 25.9 (Hab 1.15; 3.18). - Ps 2.11; Hos 10.5 are not counted;
they mean "fear, tremble" (from√גיל?; see my remarks, HUCA 24
[1952 f.] p. 111). - The alternative 20/-:- or -/18:- and
-:20/- or -:-/22 depends on whether or not the passages in the
parentheses are regarded as psalm passages.

      90   Note that with the preposition על the ratio is
5+1 prose:1 (13.6; 103.10; 116.7; 119.17; 142.8. Prose

2 Ch 20.11), while with other prepositions, suffixes, or a direct object it is 5:9 (7.5; 18.21; 137.8; Isa 63.7 [bis]).

91   3.4; 18.3, 31; 28.7; 33.20; 59.12; 84.12; 115.9; 119.114; 144.2. In 7.11 and 18.36, which are not counted, the word has a religious meaning, too. J.H. Patton, Canaanite Parallels in the Book of Psalms, 1944, p. 41, assumes √מחן with the meaning "beseech, do homage" as in Ugaritic (also known from Aramaic and Arabic) in a number of the above listed psalm passages. This is at best possible only in 7.11.

92   a) Verb 5:1 (35.5; 36.13; 62.4; 118.13; 140.5). b) Substantives: דֳחִי 1:0 (56.14); מִדְחָה 0:1. The participle (־יִשְׂרָאֵל)נִדְחֵי (147.2; outside Isa 11.12; 56.8) is identical with נִדָּחַי (Jer 49.36) and belongs to √נדח (GB, p. 160; GK § 20 m).

93   1.2; 2.1; 35.28; 37.30; 38.13; 63.7; 71.24; 77.13; 115.7; 143.5; Isa 38.14 (Isa 59.11. Reading 'וְהֹגֹה' [Isa 59.13] instead of MT וְהֹגֹה or understanding it as a Qal would add another alternative figure to the ratio; cf. n. 89.).- It is hard to break the verb up into more accurate meanings, as the limits are vague. Mere uttering of a sound by man or beast is according to a) LVT, p. 224, 1:2, b) GB, p. 173, 1:4. This would leave for the meanings "think" and "speak" (GB) the ratios s) 11(12)/10:7/8(9); b) 11(12)/10:5(6)/7.

94   21.6; 96.6; 104.1; 111.3. This combination of the two words is psalm language, whereas הוד alone is 8:13 and הָדָר alone is 11:17.

95   Sing. 52.9; pl. 5.10; 38.13; 52.4; 55.12; 57.2;
91.3; 94.20. The total of psalm occurrences would not be
changed if, following S, we were to drop 52.9 and add 74.19
for חיה[1] (while the ratio in the psalms of pl. to sing.
would be a clear 8:0). The total of the outside occurrences
cannot so easily be given. The parenthesized -(6) add the
two Qeres (Job 6.2; 30.13) to the -:4-, which latter,in turn,
include Prov 11.6 (against LVT, p. 228).

96   With קשר 5.8; 79.1; 138.2; Jonah 2.5, 8.
With קשרו 11.4. Cf. No. 116.

97   38.7; 55.15; 81.14; 85.14; 86.11; 89.16; 104.3,
10, 26; 115.7; 131.1; 142.4; Lam 5.18 (Isa 59.9; Hab 3.11).
For the alternative ratios cf. n. 89.

98   19.14; 86.14. In addition, this word is found
six times in Ps 119. Emend זרים of Isa 25.2 (G), 5 (G, T;
cf. the parallelism עָרִיצִים–זֵדִים in 13.11). זרים is written
for זדים also in Ps 54.5, as the almost identical verse 86.14
shows. An error of a similar kind is indicated in No. 53. -
The sing. occurs once, outside.

99   6.6; 9.7; 30.5; 34.17; 97.12; 102.13; 109.15;
111.4; 112.6; 135.13; 145.7; Isa 26.8, 14.

100   43.2; 44.10, 24; 60.3, 12; 74.1; 77.8; 88.15;
89.39. - Hos 8.5 is not counted. It probably means "be fat";
cf. והרי זנחתי (Tanḥuma Balaq and Num. Rabba to 23.10).

101   Piel 22.30; 30.4; 33.19; 41.3; 71.20; 80.19;
85.7; 138.7; 143.11; 1 Sam 2.6; Hab 3.2. Prose Ne 9.6.

In addition, the _Piel_ is found eleven times in Ps 119, of which it appears nine times in the form חָנֵּנִי. Of the outside material, Ne 3.34 is not counted. It means "assemble" as in Zech 10.9; 'Nu 24.23' (for the text cf. W.F. Albright, JBL 63 [1944], p. 222, n. 108) and Phen., Sl. 4.2. - _Hiphil_ Isa 38.16. The ratios state that the psalms use the _Piel_ 10 to 20 times as much as the _Hiphil_ (depending on how much is allowed for the repetitions in Ps 119), while the rest of the Bible uses it only 1½ times as much. The meaning of both stems is identical, notwithstanding the attempt of LVT, p. 293, to detect differences.

102   _Qal_ 0:1. _Niphal_ 1:2 (60.7). _Piel_ 9:1 (6.5; 18.20; 34.8; 50.15; 91.15; 116.8; 119.153; 140.2). - The numeration of the root follows GB. The etymology of the sequence of the consonants חלץ is disputed. GB, p. 236, has three different roots; LVT, p. 305, assumes only one root. At any rate, biblical speakers and writers were hardly conscious of any connection among the three basic meanings of the verb(s) חלץ.

103   4.2; 6.3; 9.14; 25.16; 26.11; 27.7; 30.11; 31.10; 41.5, 11; 51.3; 56.2; 57.2; 59.6; 67.2; 77.10; 86.3, 16; 102.14; 119.29, 58, 132; 123.2 f.; Isa 26.10; 33.2. Of these 26:- times, 20 are חָנֵּנִי, חָנְנֵנִי, חָנַּנִי.

104   37.21, 26; 109.12; 112.5. All four mean "support". Three (37.21, 26; 112.5) are from wisdom psalms.

105   _Poel_ 1:1 (102.15). _Piel_, _Hitpael_ 2+2 prose: 7 (30.9; 142.2. Prose 1 Ki 8.33, 47). Jer 22.23 (_Niphal_?) is

uncertain; not counted.

106   4.4; 12.2; 16.10; 18.26; 30.5; 31.24; 32.6;
37.28; 43.1; 50.5; 52.11; 79.2; 85.9; 86.2; 89.20; 97.10;
116.15; 132.9, 16; 145.10, 17; 148.10; 149.1, 5, 9; 1 Sam 2.9.
Vocalize 'חֲסִידֶ֫ךָ' Dt 33.8 (against F.E. König, Historisch-
kritisches Lehrgebäude der hebräischen Sprache II 2, 1897,
p. 403). - Twice חסיד is a divine epithet (145.17; Jer 3.12).
The two remaining passages outside of the psalms (Mi 7.2;
Prov 2.8) where חסיד refers to man are closely related to the
psalms (cmp. Ps 12.2; 1 Sam 2.9). This makes the word virtually an exclusive psalm term.

107   Cf. No. 44 and n. 78.

108   The following occurrences are not counted because
of the difficulties of the texts or of ambiguities in the
meanings: 52.3; 89.3; 101.1; 141.5; Prov 14.34. Gen 19.19
is included in +12:-. 1 Sam 20.14; 2 Sam 9.3 are included
in -:57, as is Dt 33.8 (cf. the preceding note), although in
the latter case a different arrangement is conceivable, interpreting the pronominal suffix 'חֲסִידֶ֫ךָ' as a genitivus subjectivus.

109   2.12; 5.12; 7.2; 11.1; 16.1; 17.7; 18.3, 31;
25.20; 31.2, 20; 34.9, 23; 36.8; 37.40; 57.2 (bis); 61.5;
64.11; 91.4; 118.8 f.; 141.8; 144.2; Na 1.7. - Prov 30.5 is
a quotation from Ps 18.31; not counted. All the psalm passages
and six outside passages speak of men who strive to, or do, חסה
by God (Dt 32.37 by foreign gods). Twice (Ju 9.15; Isa 30.2)
the word is used in a nonreligious sense. Cf. No. 73.

110   14.6; 46.2; 61.4; 62.9; 71.7; 91.2, 9; 94.22; 142.6; Isa 25.4; Jer 17.17. In addition, the word is used in a general religious sense 62.8; 73.28.

111   104.18 and the two references at the end of the preceding note.

112   68.5, 19; 77.12; 89.9; 94.7, 12; 102.19; 115.17 f.; 118.5, 14, 17, 18, 19; 122.4; 130.3; 135.4; 150.6; Isa 38.11. חַלְלוּיָהּ, whether written in one word or in two (135.3), is not counted; cf. n. 203. Nor is Isa 26.4; text? In Isa 38.11, יהּ of MT (editions) is supported against יהוה of mss., versions by 1QIs[a] which has only one יהּ. There is some doubt as to text and meaning of כֵּס־יָהּ (Ex 17.16).

113   31.25; 33.18, 22; 69.4; 71.14; 130.7; 131.3; 147.11; Job 14.14. In addition, this word is found five times in Ps 119, with יְיַחֵלְנוּ in v. 49 not counted.

114   16.11; 17.7; 18.36; 20.7; 44.4; 48.11; 60.7; 63.9; 74.11; 77.11; 78.54; 80.16, 18; 98.1; 110.1; 118.15, 16 (only one is counted); 138.7; 139.10. In all these occurrences, יָמִין is a metaphor for God's (right) hand. In addition to the -:4, there are three passages in which יָמִין of God means His right side (e.g. Zech 3.1).

115   15.4; 22.24; 66.16; 115.11, 13; 118.4; 135.20. - But the sing. יְרֵא יהוה/אֱלֹהִים/יִרְאַת is not a psalm term: its ratio is 3:9 (95.12; 128.1, 4). - Cf. No. 12.

116   65.6; 106.22; 139.14; 145.6; Isa 64.2. Prose 2 Sam 7.23

93

117   9.9; 17.2; 58.2; 75.3; 96.10; 98.9; 99.4; Isa 26.7.
Prose 1 Ch 29.17. Prov 23.31 and Cant 7.10 are not counted.
There the word describes the wine. For a similar reason,
Cant 1.4 is doubtful (this is indicated by the alternative
ratio -:7/8.); note that יִין precedes.

118   7.10; 8.4; 9.8; 21.13; 24.2; 40.3; 48.9; 68.10;
90.17 (bis); 99.4; 119.30; Ex 15.17. Prose 2 Sam 7.24.

119   7.13; 11.2; 37.23; 59.5; 87.5; 107.36; 119.73.

120   33.14; 89.15; 97.2; 104.5; Ex 15.17; 1 Ki 8.13.
Prose 1 Ki 8.39, 43, 49.

121   38.17; 46.3, 7; 55.23; 60.4; 66.9; 94.18; 121.3.

122   10.6; 13.5; 15.5; 16.6; 17.5; 21.8; 30.7; 46.6;
62.3, 7; 82.5; 93.1; 96.10; 104.5; 112.6; 125.1. (Possibly
140.11 [Qere]; text? The expression is similar to that of
the Hiphil 55.4) Although there seems to be no difference in
meaning between the Qal and the Niphal, the psalms plainly
prefer the Niphal.

123   Hiphil 55.4.

124   2.2; 76.13; 89.28; 138.4; 148.11. Cf. No. 48.

125   19.3; 59.8; 78.2; 94.4; 119.171; 145.7. This
meaning is semantically set apart from "flow, make flow",
whether or not one follows GB, p. 481, in assuming a separate
root II נבע .

126   47.10; 83.12; 107.40; 113.8 (bis); 118.9; 146.3;
1 Sam 2.8. The ratio of the sing. is 0:11 (0:12 with Cant 6.12.
But that passage [6.12b-7.1] is probably to be read. שָׂם אֲנִי מֶרְךָּ '

בֵּת עֲאִינְדָבּ' שׁוּבִי שׁוּבִי', שׁוּבִי הַשּׁוּלַמִּית at the suggestion of N.H. Tur-
Sinai, <u>Halashon wehasefer</u> II, 1950 f., pp. 385 f.

    127   28.9; 33.12; 74.2; 78.62, 71; 94.5, 14; 106.5,
40; Isa 63.17; Joel 2.17; Mi 7.14, 18. Prose Dt 9.26, 29;
1 Ki 8.36, 51. It is possible that נחלה is a metaphor for
Israel in one or more of the following outside passages:
1 Sam 26.19; Jer 12.7, 8, 9.

    128   9.7, 19; 10.11; 13.2; 16.11; 44.24; 49.20; 52.7;
68.17; 74.1, 3, 10, 19; 77.9; 79.5; 89.47; 103.9; Isa 33.20;
Jer 15.18; Job 14.20; Lam 5.20 (Hab 1.4; cf. n. 89). 1 Sam 15.29
Lam 3.18; 1 Ch 29.11 have other meanings and are not counted.

    129   17.11; 18.6; 22.13, 17; 88.18; 109.3; 118.10, 11
(only one is counted), 12. All are סְבָבוּנִי or סַבּוּנִי.

    130   49.6; 71.21; 114.3, 5.

    131   7.8; 26.6; 32.7, 10; 55.11; 59.9; Jonah 2.4, 6.

    132   17.8; 27.5; 31.21; 64.3; Job 14.13.

    133   10.11; 13.2; 22.25; 27.9; 30.8; 44.25; 88.15;
102.3; 143.7; Isa 64.6; Job 13.24. <u>Niphal</u> (without פנים)
89.47. 69.18 is only a slight variant of the formula of 27.9
(102.3; 143.7); not counted. הַסְתֵּר וָאֶקְצֹף (Isa 57.17) may be added
to the outside occurrences; vocalizing as <u>Niphal</u> is possible.

    134   83.18; 92.8; 132.12, 14; Isa 26.4. Cf. Nos. 92,
99 f.

    135   9.19; 19.10; 21.7; 22.27; 37.29; 61.9; 89.30;
111.3; 112.3; 148.6; Isa 64.8; Mi 7.18.

    136   25.10; 78.56; 93.5; 99.7 (probably 132.12).

In addition, this word is found fourteen times in Ps 119.
Its identity is uncertain. It rests on the correctness of
the vocalization of the Masorah which distinguishes it
(artificially?) from עֵדוֹת. Cf. also No. 26.

137   Cf. n. 59. The lowest figure, -:(33?), refers
to the possibility of deriving Ju 9.51 from √עוֹז (cf. n. 59);
but this is not very likely. 2 Ch 30.21 is not counted, the
text being uncertain.

138   77.4; 107.5; 142.4; 143.4; Jonah 2.8.

139   7.18; 9.3; 18.14; 21.8; 46.5; 47.3; 50.14;
73.11; 77.11; 78.17; 82.6; 83.19; 91.1, 9; 92.2; 97.9; 107.11;
once in אֵל עֶלְיוֹן (78.35); twice in אֱלֹהִים עֶלְיוֹן (57.3; 78.56). -
Gen 14.18, 19, 20 are not counted, since Melchizedek's god is
meant; only v. 22, where Abram establishes the identification
of that god with his own, is counted as an outside occurrence.

140   Poel: Lam 1.22 (bis); 2.20. Poal: Lam 1.12.
Hitpoel:141.4.

141   עוֹלָם (adv.) has the ratio 5:0 (61.8; 66.7;
89.2 f., 38 [Isa 64.4, a psalm, is not counted; text?]), and
thus might constitute a separate item in the first list. -
לְעֵילֹם (2 Ch 33.7) is counted as an outside occurrence.
לְעוֹלָם is not counted in the expression לְעוֹלָם וָעֶד in this
number but in No. 99. Cf. also Nos. 100 f., 204.

142   עֹלָם וָעֶד 5:1 (10.16; 21.5; 48.15; 52.10; 104.5).
לְעוֹלָם וָעֶד 6:3 (9.6; 119.44; 145.1, 2, 21; Ex 15.18). Cf.
Nos. 91 f., 98, 100 f., 204.

143   113.2; 115.18; 121.8; 125.2; 131.3.

144   עולמים 5/6:2 (61.5; 77.6; 145.13; 1 Ki 8.13;
Isa 26.4 [Isa 51.9; see n. 89]).   לעולמים 1:1 (77.8).
עד עולמי עד 0:1.

145   עלז verb 28.7; 60.8; 68.5; 94.3; 96.12; 149.5;
Jer 15.17 (Hab 3.18; see n. 89).   עלץ verb 5.12; 9.3; 25.2;
64.4; 1 Sam 2.1.

146   √עלץ 5.12; 9.3; 25.2; 64.4; 1 Sam 2.1; 1 Ch 16.32
(Hab 3.14; see n. 89). √עלז 28.7; 60.8; 68.5; 94.3; 96.12;
149.5; Jer 15.17 (Hab 3.18). √עלס no psalm occurrences. -
Job 39.13 is not counted (meaning?). Although the tendency
of the psalms to use √עלז and of the rest of the Bible to use
√עלץ and √עלס is unmistakable, it asserts itself only with
varying consistency: 96.12 has √עלז, while the parallel text
1 Ch 16.32 has √עלץ.

147   77.12; 77.15; 78.12; 88.11, 13; 89.6; 119.129;
Ex 15.11; Isa 25.1. - Lam 1.9 is not counted, as its meaning
is different. Cf. Nos. 30, 104.

148   9.2; 26.7; 40.6; 71.17; 72.18; 75.2; 78.4, 11,
32; 86.10; 96.3; 98.1; 105.2, 5; 106.7, 22; 107.8, 24; 111.4;
119.18, 27; 136.4; 145.5; Mi 7.15. Prose Ne 9.17. Not counted
because of different meanings: 131.1; Job 42.3; Dan 8.24; 11.36.

149   17.13; 18.3, 44, 49; 22.5, 9; 31.2; 37.40 (bis);
40.18; 43.1; 56.8; 71.4; 82.4; 91.14; 144.2   (32.7 text?,
meaning?). Job 21.10 has a different meaning; not counted.

150   5.6; 6.9; 7.14, 16; 11.3; 14.4; 15.2; 28.3; 31.20;

36.13; 58.3; 59.3; 64.3; 68.29; 74.12; 92.8, 10; 94.4, 16;
101.8; 119.3; 125.5; 141.4, 9; Ex 15.17; Isa 26.12; Job 7.20. -
The paranomastic expressions 44.2 and Hab 1.5 are not entered
here, since they are counted in No.107; cf. p. 6.

    151   9.17; 44.2; 64.10; 77.13; 90.16; 92.5; 95.9;
111.3; 143.5; Dt 32.4; Hab 3.2.

    152   28.5.

    153   46.9.

    154   17.5; 57.7; 58.11; 74.3; 85.14; 119.133; 140.5;
Isa 26.6. The parenthesized -:...(5) refers to Ju 5.28, whose
meaning is not clear.

    155   68.23; 69.3, 16; 88.7; 107.24; Ex 15.5; Mi 7.19;
Jonah 2.4. Prose Ne 9.11.

    156   18.3, 32, 47; 19.15; 28.1; 31.3; 62.3, 8; 73.26;
78.35; 89.27; 92.16; 94.22; 95.1; 144.1; Dt 32.4; 1 Sam 2.2;
Isa 26.4.

    157   72.16; 90.6; 92.8; 103.15 (132.18. In this
passage the word might be denominated from the צִיץ of the
high priest; consequently, it would not belong here).

    158   18.7; 31.10; 59.17; 66.14; 69.18; 102.3; 106.44;
107.6; 119.143; Isa 25.4; 26.16; Job 7.11; Lam 1.20. Job 36.16
is possibly 113) II צר, "adversary" (apposition to רַהַב, "hell";
cf. partly B. Szold, Sefer 'iyov (Das Buch Hiob), 1886, p. 419.).
Not counted: Isa 5.28; Job 41.7, both mean צר, "flint".
Job 36.19 is uncertain. - Cf. No. 209.

    159   3.2; 13.5; 27.2, 12; 44.6, 8, 11; 60.13 f.;

74.10; 78.42, 61, 66; 81.15; 89.24, 43; 97.3; 105.24; 106.11;
107.2; 112.8; 119.139, 157; 136.24; Gen 14.20; Isa 26.11;
63.18; 64.1; Na 1.2; Lam 1.10. Prose Ne 9.27. Not counted
(text?) Jer 48.5; Ez 30.16. The alternative depends upon
the interpretation of Job 36.16; cf. the preceding note.

      160   6.8; 7.5, 7; 8.3; 10.5; 23.5; 31.12; 42.11;
69.20; 74.4, 23; 143.12.

      161   17.13; 18.6, 19; 21.4; 59.11; 68.26; 79.8; 88.14;
89.15; 95.2; 119.147 f. - Ne 13.2 is a quotation from Dt 23.5;
not counted. Twenty forms are Piel; the remaining two, both
outside, are Hiphil.

      162   שֵׁם קָדְשׁוֹ 4:0 (33.21; 103.1; 105.3; 145.21); הַר קׇ'
3:0 (3.5; 48.2; 99.9); זָכַר קׇ' 2:0 (30.5; 97.12); רוּחַ קׇ' 2:0
(Isa 63.10 f.; cf. No. 35); מָקוֹם קׇ' 1+1 prose:0 (24.3. Prose
Ezra 9.8); מָרוֹם קׇ' 1:0 (47.9); בָּא קׇ' 1:0 (78.54); גְּבוּל קׇ' 1:0
(102.20); שְׁמֵי קׇ' 1:0 (20.7); דְּבַר/דִּבְרֵי קׇ' 1:1 (105.42); זְרוֹעַ קׇ'
1:1 (98.1); הֵיכַל קׇ' 1:2 (11.4; cf. No. 62) מָעוֹן קׇ' 1:3
(68.6). - While קׇדְשֶׁךָ is natural in prayer and קׇדְשִׁי in the
divine speech which is found chiefly in the Prophets, קׇדְשׁוֹ
might not be expected to have any leaning toward the psalms or
any other type of biblical literature.

      163   Qal 3:3 (25.3; 37.9; 69.7). Piel 20/18 :15/17
(25.5, 21; 27.14 [bis]; 37.34; 39.8; 40.2; 52.11; 56.7; 69.21;
119.95; 130.5 [bis]; Isa 25.9; 26.8; 33.2; 64.2; Jer 14.22.
[Isa 59.9, 11; cf. n.89]. Prose Gen 49.18. Jer 14.19 is
identical with 8.15; not counted).

164   18.40, 49; 44.6; 74.23; Ex 15.7; Lam 3.62.
(Jer 51.1 not counted.)   Only those occurrences are counted
where the nominal function of the participle becomes manifest
through its possessive suffixes (קָמַי etc.).   The verbal
aspect (קָמִים עָלַי) is not taken into consideration.

165   ראה Qal 22.18; 54.9; 112.8; 118.7.   Hiphil
59.11.   הביט 92.12.

166   65.10; 120.6; 123.4; 129.1 f.

167   Polel 4:0 (9.14; 18.49; 27.5; 1 Sam 2.7).   Hiphil
4:2 (3.4 with רֹאשִׁי object; 75.8; 89.20; 113.7).   89.43 not
counted.

168   75.5 f., 11; 89.18, 25; 92.11; 112.9; 148.14;
1 Sam 2.1, 10.   The meaning of 1 Ch 25.5 is not clear; it is
not counted.

169   32.2; 52.4; 101.7; 120.2 f. - The alternative
refers to קֶשֶׁת רְמִיָּה (78.57; Hos 7.11) which may be either
"treacherous" or "slack bow".

170   22.17; 26.5; 27.2; 37.1, 9; 64.3; 92.12; 94.16;
119.115; Jer 20.13.   (The sing. is 0:2, which would bring the
ratio to 10:8.)   37.1 and Prov 24.19 are almost identical.
Since dependency could not be established for either passage,
both are counted.

171   a) 4:2 (104.27; 119.166; 145.15; Isa 38.18).
b) 2:0 (119.116; 146.5).

172   20.2; 59.2; 69.30; 91.14; 107.41 (all factitive
[Piel].   Outside Prov 18.10; 29.25 [Job 5.11?]; all stative

or passive).

173   38.21; 71.13; 109.4, 20, 29.

174   55.18; 69.13; 77.4, 7, 13; 105.2; 143.5; 145.5; Job 7.11. In addition, the word occurs six times in Ps 119.

175   The plural prevails (8:3). Sing. 55.13. Pl. 18.41; 44.8, 11; 68.2; 81.16; 83.3; 89.24; 139.21. - Note that שׁוֹא has the ratio 14:39.

176   16.8; 21.6; 89.20; 119.30. 18.34 may belong to I √שׁוה, "make like". Isa 38.13 is not clear; not counted.

177   a) "Pit" 5:3 (7.16; 9.16; 35.7; 94.13; Job 9.31 [or to b) ?]); b) "hell" 7:8 (16.10; 30.10; 49.10; 55.24; 103.4; Isa 38.17; Jonah 2.7).

178   44.14; 79.12; 80.7; 89.42.

179   43.3; 84.2; 132.5, 7. For 46.5 either the meaning of the sing. (M. Buttenwieser, The Psalms, 1938, p. 513) or of the pl. (H. Schmidt, Die Psalmen, 1934, p. 87 f.) is possible, but the sing. is preferred, since מִקְדְּשֵׁי אֵל (73.17) is a synonymous and formally identical expression, and there a plurality of sanctuaries is most unlikely. In all psalm occurrences the Temple in Jerusalem is meant. In the two outside occurrences (Job 21.28; 39.6) the meaning is profane.

180   9.9; 18.16; 19.5; 24.1; 33.8; 50.12; 77.19; 89.12; 90.2; 93.1; 96.10, 13; 97.4; 98.7, 9; 1 Sam 2.8; Isa 26.9, 18; Na 1.5.

181   33.7; 71.20; 77.17; 78.15; 106.9; 107.26; 135.6; 148.7; Ex 15.5, 8; Isa 63.13. The notion of the dual (or the

pl.) underlies 42.8.

182   Since neither GB nor LVT differentiate homonymous
roots of עזר, the present numeration must be explained. I√עזר
conveys the idea of "help". Its first radical corresponds to
Arabic ع, its second to Arabic ذ, Aram. ד; cf. GB, p. 578.
II√עזר means "behave in a manly way, be a hero" with its
derivations. It occurs in 89.20; 1 Ch 5.20; 12.1; 2 Ch 26.15.
Its first radical corresponds to Ug. ġ; cf. H.L. Ginsberg,
JBL 57 (1938), pp. 210 f., n. 5; W.F. Albright, BASOR 94 (1944),
p. 32, n. 3; UH § 18.1560. There is probably a third root,
III√עזר, meaning "withhold". Its first radical corresponds
to Arabic ع, its second to) ; cf. LVT, p. 695. It underlies
עֲזָרָה, "enclosire, yard".

183   12.6; 18.3, 36, 47; 20.7; 24.5; 25.5; 27.1, 9;
50.23; 51.14; 62.8; 65.6; 69.14; 79.9; 85.5, 8, 10; 95.1;
132.16; 1 Ch 16.35; (Hab 3.13 [the first time; the text of
the second is not certain], 18; cf. n. 89).

184   The alternative ratios depend on the inclusion
of Isa 59.11 and/or Hab 3.18 in the psalm material or their
exclusion therefrom.

185   18.51; 28.8; 42.6; 44.5; 53.7; 74.12; 116.13;
Isa 26.18. The one outside occurrence is Isa 33.6, which is
part of a liturgy (cf. H. Gunkel, ZAW 41 [1924], pp. 177-208)
though hardly a psalm itself.

186   ישׁוּעָה and ישׁוּעוֹת mean exactly the same. The
difference is one of form, not of content. Using or not

using either one is a stylistic peculiarity; therefore each
form is entered separately.

187   68.21

188   33.17; 37.39; 38.23; 40.11, 17; 51.16; 60.13;
71.15; 119.41, 81; 144.10; 146.3; 2 Ch 6.41.

189   In Rabbinic Hebrew the word ישועה , though well
known, has become so odd and תשועה comes so naturally that
the Midrash replaces the former by the latter in an
otherwise verbal citation from Ps 3.3: רבים שהיו רבים בתורה
אומרים לנפשי אומרים לדוד אדם ששבה את הכבשה והרג את הרועה והפיל
את ישראל בחרב יש לו תשועה אין ישועתה לו באלהים, "Great ones,
[i.e.] who were great in the Tora, were saying to me, [i.e.]
were saying to David [see v.1]: Is there salvation _for_ a man
who robbed the lamb and killed the shepherd and felled Israel with
the sword [referring to 2 Sam 11 f.]? There is no salvation
for him in God!" The continuation of this Midrash again
replaces ישועה by תשועה (Pesikta de R. Kahana, ed. Buber, 1868,
fol. 10b, and the parallels [with occasional variants]:
Tanḥuma, Tisa § 4; Tanḥuma, ed. Buber, 1885, Tisa, p. 106;
Midrash Tehillim, ed. Buber 1891, p. 38 [has חנפה instead of
תשועה]; Pesikta Rabbati, ed. Friedmann, 1880, fol. 39a [has
אין לזה ישועה מעתה and in the continuation עמידה אין לאלו מעתה
ולא ישועה; obviously inferior variants]).

190   P. 24, No. 158

191   ישועה -ל 3.9; 118.14, 21 (and two outside occurrences 2 Sam 10.11; Job 13.16). ישועתה ל- 3.3; 80.3; Jonah 2.10.

192   See No. 137.

193   Cf. J. Weingreen, VT 4 (1954), p. 53.

194   יֵ֫שַׁע 9/8:2/3 (18.47; 24.5; 25.5; 27.9; 65.6; 79.9; 85.5; 1 Ch 16.35 [Hab 3.18; cf. n. 89]; outside Isa 17.10; Mi 7.7); יְשׁוּעָה 2:0 (88.2; Isa 12.2 [this passage has אֵל‐ and not אֱלֹהָי‐ which is common in this phrase]). תְּשׁוּעָה 1:0 (51.16).

195   עֶזְרָתָה ל‐ Jer 37.7; עֶזְרָת ל‐ Ps 60.13. עֶזְרָה ל‐ 44.27; 63.8; 94.17. The exception is וְלֹא לְעֶזְרָה לֹו (2 Ch 28.21). The style of Chronicles in general and of this paragraph in particular is hardly typical of biblical Hebrew; cf. vv. 22b, 23b.

196   22.20; 38.23; 40.14.

197   P. 64.

198   But see nn. 201, 208.

199   16.7; 26.12; 34.2; 63.5; 66.8; 68.27; 96.2; 100.4; 103.1 f., 22; 104.1, 35; 113.2; 115.18; 132.15; 134.1 f.; 135.19; 145.1 f., 10, 21. Not counted 103.21, 22 (second time); 135.19 (second time), 20 (both times). The alternative ‐:11/12 refers to Job 2.9 where בֵּרֵךְ may have either a direct or a euphemistical meaning.

200   Ne 9.5; 1 Ch 17.27. ‐ The participle בָּרוּךְ with God as subject must always be prayer. Therefore, it would make no sense to include it in the list. It may be noted, however, that it is not as frequent in poetry as it is in prose. (It should be kept well in mind that poetical prayers ["psalms"] are much more frequent than prose prayers.) For " בָּרוּךְ is God"

the ratio between poetry and prose is 15:17 (poetry 18.47; 28.6; 31.22; 41.14; 66.20; 68.20, 36; 72.18 f.; 89.53; 118.26; 119.12; 124.6; 135.21; 144.1).

201   The sum total of occurrences, including those which do not refer to God, is given in parentheses.

202   18.4; 48.2; 96.4; 113.3; 145.3. - 78.63 is not counted.

203   104-106; 111-113; 115-117; 135 (including that of v. 3; cf. n. 112); 146-150.

204   Hab 3.3 means "splendor"; not counted.

205   95.2; 119.54. Both 2 Sam 23.1 and Isa 25.5 belong, contrary to the dictionaries, to III √זמר (cf. ﺿﻢ, "strong"). Job 35.10 is of unknown meaning and not counted.

206   81.3; 98.5.

207   Only in psalm headings.

208   The Bible uses this root solely in a religious sense with the possible but unlikely exception of Isa 24.16. There the object is the צדיק which seems to be an epithet of God, as is probably the case in Job 34.17 and possibly in Prov 21.12.

209   28.2, 6; 31;23; 86.6; 116.1; 130.2; 140.7; 143.1. Prose Dan 9.17 f.; 2 Ch 6.21 (where the parallel 1 Ki 8.30 has תחנה).

210   The passage הודו ליהוה פי טוב is counted only once, but its variations, inasmuch as they are not identical with one another, every time.

211   26.7; 42.5; 69.31; 95.2; 100.4; 147.7; Jonah 2.10.

212   50.14, 23; 56.13; 107.22; 116.17. A clear distinction between prayer of thanksgiving and thanksoffering cannot
always be made.

213   The outside occurrences are Jos 7.19; Ezra 10.11.

214   Occurring Ne 12.31-40; outside.

215   30.2; 34.4; 99.5, 9; 107.32; 118.28; 145.1;
Ex 15.2; Isa 25.1. (Ps 66.17 is clear as to its general meaning
but not as to its form.) Prose Ne 9.5.

216   35.27; Isa 12.6; 42.11; 44.23. Isa 61.7 (outside)
is doubtful; text?

217   5.12; 20.6; 33.1; 51.16; 59.17; 67.5; 71.23;
84.3; 89.13; 90.14; 92.5; 95.1; 96.12; 98.4, 8; 132.9, 16;
145.7; 149.5; Isa 26.19 (Ps 63.8 text?).

218   32.11; 65.9; 81.2.

219   רָנִּי (32.7) and רְנָנִים (Job 39.13) are not counted.
The first because of the corrupt text, the second because its
relationship to our root is etymologically not clear and
semantically not existent.

220   17.1; 30.6; 42.5; 47.2; 61.2; 88.3; 105.43; 106.44;
107.22; 118.15; 119.169; 126.2, 5 f.; 142.7; Isa 44.23. Prose
1 Ki 8.28.

221   63.6; 100.2.

222   The neutral meaning of this root, "call, shout",
is rare (1 Ki 22.36; Prov 1.20; 8.3; all outside). The common
meaning of √רנן is either "rejoice" or, less frequently,

"entreat, lament". - Except for two outside occurrences (Prov 1.20; 8.3), no difference in meaning is discernible between the Qal and the Piel. But even after leaving these two out, it is clear that the Piel is psalm language (20/21:5) and the Qal is not (4:12/13).

223   Piel 4:2 (63.4; 117.1; 145.4; 147.12). Hitpael 1:0 (106.47). ·

224   5.3; 18.7, 42; 22.25; 28.2; 30.3; 31.23; 72.12; 88.14; 119.147; Jonah 2.3; Job 30.20 (Hab 1.2; cf. n. 89).

225   18.7; 34.16; 39.13; 40.2; 102.2; 145.19; Lam 3.56. שׁוע (Job 30.24; 36.19) is of uncertain etymology and meaning; not counted.

226   13.6; 21.14; 27.6; 33.3; 57.8; 59.17; 65.14; 68.5, 33; 89.2; 96.1 (bis), 2; 98.1; 101.1; 104.33; 105.2; 106.12; 137.3 f.; 138.5; 144.9; 149.1; Ex 15.2; Ju 5.3; Isa 42.10 Jer 20.13. In -:8 the passive Qal Isa 26.1 is included

227   33.2; 81.3; 92.4; 98.5 (bis); 147.7; 149.3; 150.3. The three additional cases, referred to by (11):-, are 43.4; 57.9; 71.22. There the psalmist speaks of himself as praising God with the כנור. Yet it is reasonable to suppose that it is not he who sings and, at the same time, accompanies himself with the instrument, but rather that he commissions Temple musicians for the instrumental part of his service or that he joins a general prayer. Of such prayer an example is Ps 107. - The outside occurrences are 1 Sam 10.5; Isa 5.12; 24.8 (Gen 31.27?; Job 21.12?).

228   What seems to be an exception, viz. 137.2,
actually is not. It would be bad style to use the sing. of
the instruments to be hung on a plurality of poplars. -
1 Ki 10.12 is not counted, since the pl. has no collective
meaning.

229   33.2; 81.3; 92.4; 150.3. Two of the additional
cases, referred to in parentheses, are 57.9 and 144.9; cf.
n. 227. - 71.22 has נֵ֫בֶל כְּלִי‏. - The outside occurrences are
1 Sam 10.5; Isa 5.12 (Am 6.5?).

230   1 Ki 10.12 not counted; cf. n. 228.

231   עֲשׂוֹר is either an apposition (genitive?) of
(33.2; 144.9), or a parallel to (92.4), נבל .

232   81.3; 149.3; 150.4. Outside occurrences are
1 Sam 10.5; Isa 5.12 (Gen 31.27?; Job 21.12?).

233   Ez 28.13 is not counted.

234   At first it seems difficult to decide whether
מחול ,מחולה is an instrument (√חלל; cmp. חָלִיל) or a dance
(possibly a place for dancing;√חול). Passages such as
149.3; 150.4 favor the first interpretation, passages such as
Ju 21.21 the second. Nor does postbiblical usage make a
decision easy. The first meaning is manifestly present in the
following passage from the Mekhilta deR. Shimon ben Yohay, ed.
D. Hoffmann, 1905, p. 71 (to Ex 15.20; parallels with slight
variants, of which the important ones are noted here, are
Mekhilta deR. Yishmael, tract. Shiretha, and Pirke deR. Eliezer
42): וכי מאין היו להם לישראל תופים (var.) ומחולות (על הים

אלא לפי שהצדיקים מובטחין עם יציאתן ממצרים שהמקום עושה

להם נסים וגבורות על הים ולפיכך נטלו תופים ומחולות בידם

(var.) התקינו להם תופים ומחולות), "From where did the Israelites

have drums (var. and מחולות) at the (Red) Sea (var. in the

wilderness)? The righteous had been promised at the time

of their exodus from Egypt that God would perform miracles

and wonders at the sea; therefore they took drums and מחולות

in their hands (var. prepared drums and מחולות)." The second

meaning was in the mind of the Tanna who tells us (<u>Bab. Taanith</u>

31a): עתיד הקדוש ברוך הוא לעשות מחול (var. חולה)(לצדיקים

והוא יושב ביניהן בגן עדן, "The Holy One, Blessed Be He, will

make a מחול (var. חולה) for the righteous, and He will sit among

them in the Garden of Eden." In view of these conflicting

usages, a third interpretation of the word must be sought.

The root of מחולis חול, "move in a circle", hence "dance".

The substantive מחול, "dance" then assumed the meaning of

"open flat place where dances are performed" (cf. מחול הכרם,

"ground surrounding the vineyard," important occurence <u>Kil'ayim</u>

4.2). It finally came to mean "instruments played for dance

music," with the earlier meanings still in use at the time of

the later one. The same semantic development occured to

ὀρχήστρα, "place where dances are performed" (from ὀρχέομαι,

"I dance"), which has become the modern "orchestra"; or to χορός

originally "place for dancing, dance" (from χορεύω "I dance"),

then the antique and modern "chorus". - At any rate, whatever the

meaning of מחול or מחולה in a particular passage may be, the use

of their sing. and pl., respectively, in the various types
of biblical literature justifies their listing here.

235   30.12; 149.3; 150.4; Lam 5.15. Outside occurrences
are Jer 31.3, 12; Cant 7.1.

236   The list of musical instruments mentioned in the
psalms is completed on p. 63. In this note only a few remarks
are made about those words for instruments occurring in the
psalms which use the pl. for the collective, at first sight
not conforming to the law of psalm language, as it has become
apparent in Nos. 148-152, which requires the sing. for the
collective.

צֶלְצְלִים 1(2):1 (150.5) is pl. tantum similar to (the dual)
מְצִלְתַּיִם or English "cymbals", as the instrument consists of two
plates.

מִנִּים 1:0 (150.4) is likewise pl. tantum, as several
strings make up one instrument.

חֲצֹצְרוֹת 1:28 (98:6); see n. 468.

237   בַּעֲדֵנִי 1:0 (139.11); תַּחְתֵּנִי 3:0 (2 Sam 22.37, 40,
48; Ps 18 has the usual תַּחְתָּי instead).

238   With substantives 7:4 (103.3 [bis], 4 f.; 116.7,
19; 135.9; outside 2 Ki 4.3, 7 [bis]; Jer 11.15). With verbs
2:0 (103.4; 137.6). With prepositions 1:1 (עָלַיְכִי 116.7;
outside לְכִי 2 Ki 4.2).

239   See GK § 103 f, n. 3.

240   17.10; 21.11; 89.18.

241   17.10; 58.7; 59.13.

242   2.3; 11.7; 35.16; 49.12; 58.7; 59.13; 73.7; 83.12; 140.4, 10.

243   59.14; 73.5.

244   2.4; 28.8; 44.4, 11; 49.14; 55.20; 56.8; 58.5, 8; 59.9; 64.6 (bis); 66.7; '73.3' (read ‏לָמוֹ אֵם‎'), 6, 10, 18; 78.24, 66; 80.7; 88.9; 99.7; 119.165; Dt 33.2 (bis); Isa 26.14, 16; Job 14.21; Lam 1.22.

245   2.5.

246   5.12; 55.16; 64.9.

247   ‏מוֹ‎ 2.5; 5.11; 21.10, 13; 22.5; 59.12; 73.6; 80.6; 83.12; 140.10; Ex 15.7, 9 (bis), 10, 12, 15, 17 (bis); outside Ex 23.31; Ps 45.17.   ‏מִי‎ Ex 15.5.

248   74.2; 78.54; 104.8, 26; Isa 25.9.

249   9.16; 10.2; 17.9; 31.5; 32.8; 62.12; 68.29; 142.4; 143.8; Ex 15.13, 16 (Hab 1.11; cf. n. 89).

250   132.12.

251   ‏הַמָּוְתָה‎ 1:0 (116.15); ‏נַחְלָה‎ 1:0 (124.4); ‏הַחַשְׁמַלָה‎ 0:1 (Ez 8.2); ‏אַרְצָה‎ 0:1/2 (Job 34.13; 37.12 [the vocalization is doubtful; '‏אַרְצֹה‎' is quite possible in view of Prov 8.32]).

252   ‏יְשֻׁעָתָה‎ 3:0 (3.3; 80.3; Jonah 2.10); ‏עֶזְרָתָה‎ 3:0 (44.27; 63.8; 94.17); ‏אֵימָתָה‎ 1:0 (Ex 15.16); ‏עֵפָתָה‎ 1:0 (Job 10.22); ‏צָרָתָה‎ 1:0 (120.1); ‏עַוְלָתָה‎ 1:2 (92.16 Qere; Ez 28.15; Hos 10.13); ‏סוּפָתָה‎ 0:1 (Hos 8.7); ‏מְזִמָּתָה‎ (?) 0:0/1 (Jer 11.15; text?).

253   The second figures indicate less preferable alternatives (whether or not a few very short utterances within narratives are regarded as prayers, certain repetitions counted

etc.). הָבָה was certainly not felt as a verbal form in biblical
times; not counted.

254   These two imperatives can rightly be juxtaposed
for comparison, since no difference in meaning between them
can be detected (cf. [W. Gesenius[29] -] G. Bergsträsser,
Hebräische Grammatik, 2nd part, 1929, § 10 b).

255   One would look in vain for a remark in the current
grammars verifying the fact that this or other forms are
largely determined by literary species and their traditions.
This cognition would have saved many an author from seeking
special meanings in the imperative קָטְלָה   where none exist
(cf. GK § 48 k), from ascribing it to euphony (P. Joüon,
Grammaire de l'hébreu biblique, 2nd ed., 1947, p. 109), or
from summarily calling other grammatical forms listed in this
study, "poetic" (GK, pp. 508 f.; E. König, Stilistik, Rhetorik,
Poetik..., 1900, pp. 278 ff.).

256   31.3; 71.2; 86.1; 88.3; 102.3. Prose 2 Ki 19.16;
Dan 9.18.

257   17.6; (the -:3 are from Proverbs).

258   83.18; 92.8; 104.23; 132.12, 14; 147.6; Isa 26.4.
Lengthened forms of other prepositions are characteristic of
Job: אֱלֵי, לְמוֹ, מִנִּי (עֲלֵי) .

259   47.10; 92.6; 97.9. The same order is followed
in the Mishnah רמה אֱנוֹשׁ שֶׁתִּקְוַת רוּחַ שְׁפַל הֱוֵי מְאֹד מְאֹד , "Be very,
very humble, for man's hope is vermin" (Avot 4.4). This
passage, however, is a quotation from Ecclesiasticus 7.17

(cf. n. 12); in the Mishna אישׁ is <u>hap. leg.</u>, in (the Cairo!) Ecclesiasticus it occurs quite frequently.

    260   5.8; 13.6; 26.11; 31.7, 15; 55.24; 59.17; 71.14; 109.25; 118.7; 119.87; Jer 17.16; Jonah 2.10 (Hab 3.18; cf. n. 89). Stylistically 88.14 belongs here, only the contrast is not to the wicked but to the dead; cmp. also 115.18. Somewhat similar cases are 41.13; 73.2, 28, all <u>casus pendentes</u>, and 73.2, also <u>casus pendens</u> with inverted contrast which is characteristic of this psalm. - In 2.6 the subject is God and the contrast between Him and His enemies, who are also the enemies of the psalmist (v. 2). - 30.7; 31.23; Jonah 2.5 represent another stylistic peculiarity and are listed in No. 164. One hardly finds this sort of expression in the rest of the Bible.

    261   20.8 f.; 124.7. Prose 2 Ch 20.12. (115.18, with which cmp. 88.14 and the preceding note.) In Ne 9.33, a prose prayer, the contrast in inverted somewhat as in 73.2.

    262   41.5; 82.6; 116.11; Isa 38.10.

    263   30.7; 31.23; Jonah 2.5. The (6) refers to וַאֲנִי אָמַרְתִּי (Jer 3.19).

    264   In the psalms this phrase is, with one exception (82.6), part of thanksgiving songs of individuals. With it, the "story of the thanking individual"begins (GuPs, p. 113; GuBe, pp. 268-272). 31.23 is part of vv. 20-25, a "thanksgiving song, sung in advance" (GuPs, p. 131), within a lamentation of an individual. K. Budde's remarks about אֲנִי אָמַרְתִּי

and related expressions in JBL 40 (1921), pp. 39 f., are
without bearing on our problem.

265   נַקֵּנִי...וְנִקֵּיתִי (19.13 f.); הַצִּילֵנִי...אַצִּלָה (69.15);
וְאֵרָפֵא...רְפָאֵנִי (Jer 17.14); וְאִוָּשֵׁעָה וְהוֹשִׁיעֵנִי (Jer 17.14);
וָאֵפָת...פִּתִּיתַנִי (Jer 20.7); וְאִוָּסֵר יִסַּרְתַּנִי (Jer 31.18); הֲשִׁיבֵנִי
וְאָשׁוּבָה (Jer 31.18); הֲשִׁיבֵנוּ...וְנָשׁוּבָה (Lam 5.21). It is noted
that this strain is characteristic of Jeremiah, but he, too,
uses it, with one exception (Jer 31.4), only in prayers; the
exception is God's promise to fulfill Israel's hope, its
unspoken prayer.

266   This is poetic rather than stylistic form. But
it is of a related kind, a borderline case whose omission
would do more harm than its inclusion. The occurrences are:
29.1 f., 3, 4 f.; 47.7; 67.4; 68.16; 77.2, 17; 92.10; 93.3;
94.1, 3 (23?); 96.1 f., 13; 98.5; 118.15 f.; 122.5; 124.1 f.;
129.1 f.; Ex 15.6, 11, 16; Ju 5.3, 5; Isa 25.4, 9; 26.5 (6?),
15; Hab 3.2 (8). Outside Gen 49.22; Ju 5.7, 11, 12, 19, 20,
21, 23, 27, 30; Isa 24.4, 16 (19?); 25.6, 7; 27.5; Cant 4.8,
9, 12; 7.1. Use has been made of Albright's article in Studies
in O.T. Prophecy, Presented to T.H. Robinson, ed. H.H. Rowley,
1950, pp. 5 ff., but the present list differs from Albright's,
owing to the inclusion of additional material and the exclusion
of a number of occurrences adduced by Albright. It is also at
variance with some of F. Horst's remarks in Theol. Rundschau,
N.F. 21 (1953), pp. 100 f. References with question marks
are open to different evaluations.

267   124.3, 4, 5.

268   Two occurrences are gained by emendations (58.2;
73.1; cf. BH) and one of MT eliminated (Nu 24.23; cf. Albright,
l. c. [n. 101]). - Cf. No. 43.

269   Not counting the occurrences of אל in the Book
of Job, the ratio would be 81(79)+6 prose:70/71. אל occurs
in the Book of Job 56 times. The use of divine names in that
book is singular. In its poetic part, יהוה occurs once and
אלהים 6 times, but שדי 31 times and אלה 41 times. By almost
completely avoiding the two most common biblical names or
words for God, viz. יהוה and אלהים, the Book of Job by necessity
resorts to names and words which are otherwise rare; it can,
therefore, not be regarded as normal Hebrew in this respect.
Cf. n. 272.

270   12.6; 79.11; 102.21. Also the one outside occurrence (Mal 2.13) is cultic. It is a description of a lamentation, or even a brief citation, a kind of key word.

271   8.5; 9.20 f.; 10.18; 55.14; 56.2; 66.12; 73.5;
90.3; 103.15; 104.15 (bis); 144.3; Jer 20.10; Job 7.17; 10.4,
5; 14.19. Prose 2 Ch 14.10.

272   Not counting the eighteen occurrences of אנוש in
the Book of Job, four of which are from psalm passages (cf.
n. 271), the ratio would be 14+1 prose:8. Assuming that the
Book of Job was exposed to strong Aramaic influence (to say
nothing of the hypothesis that it was translated from an Aramaic
original), אנוש might be a Hebraized אנש and its frequency in

Job thus explained. Cf. n. 269, where the influence of
Aram. אֲלָא might be noted as a further cause of the frequency
of אֱלֹהַּ in Job.

273   21.3; '61.6'.

274   7.10; 26.2; Jer 11.20 (quoted in Jer 20.12).
(Without פְּלִילוֹת in a prose prayer 1 Ch 29.17.)

275   49.11; 73.22; 92.7.

276   10.2; 31.19, 24; 36.12; 46.4; 68.35; 73.6.
Job 41.7 is not counted among -:11; text?

277   34.4; 69.31.

278   15.1; 61.5.

279   18.48; 47.4.

280   10.6; 33.11; 49.12; 61.7; 72.5; 77.9; 79.13;
85.6; 89.2, 5; 90.1 (has פְּדוֹר וָדֹר); 102.13, 25; 106.31;
119.90; 135.13; 146.10; Lam 5.19 (Isa 51.9; cf. n. 89).

281   94.17; 115.17. Cf. No. 7.

282   31.7; Jonah 2.9.

283   5.2; 39.4.

284   99.5; 110.1; 132.7.

285   50.11; 80.14.

286   50.10; 79.2; 104.11, 20.

287   17.14 (text?); 39.6; 49.2; 89.48 (text?).

288   10.8, 10, 14 (text of v. 10?).

289   74.20; 88.7, 19; 143.3 (text of 88.19?).

290   22.21; 35.17.

291   40.3; 69.3.

292   7.6; 16.9; 30.13 (read 'פְּבֹדִי', cf. LXX ἡ δόξα μου);
57.9 (outside Gen 49.6; Lam 2.11). The vocalization 'כְּבֹד'
which conveys the exact meaning was suggested by GuPs, p. 26,
and is now supported by similar phrases in Ugaritic. MT has
the correct vocalization only for Lam 2.11. J. Pedersen's
objections (Israel I-II, 1926, pp. 239, 519), followed by
H. Schmidt, Die Psalmen, 1934, p. 12, are not convincing.
But even retaining כְּבֹוד of MT, one would be justified in
singling out the above listed passages because there the
meaning of כְּבֹוד is distinct from the usual one. Cf. also
F. Nötscher, VT 2 (1952), pp. 358-362.

293   38.7 f.; Isa 64.8, 11; Lam 5.22. In addition,
the phrase is found four times in Ps 119. -:-/9 refers to
the variant עַד לִמְאֹד (2 Ch 16.14).

294   79.11; 102.21. The versions read so 34.22, too;
MT, however, is preferable.

295   18.39; 68.22; 110.5 f. (Hab 3.13; cf. n. 89).
68.24 is not counted (text?).

296   118.10, 11, 12.

297   6.7; 39.12; 147.18.

298   59.17; 142.5; 2 Sam 22.3; Jer 16.19. Cf. No. 19.

299   18.37; 26.1; 37.31; 69.24. Among the outside
occurrences, Prov 25.19 is counted.

300   16.6, 11; 133.1; 135.3; 147.1. The alternative
ratios refer to the possibility of deriving 81.3 and/or
2 Sam 23.1 from (II)√נעם, related to Middle Hebrew נְעִימָה,

"tune"; نَغَم , "sing"; تَحْلِيل , "tone, modulation" and the like; cf. GB, p. 509.

301   73.18; 74.3.

302   17.5; 23.3; 65.12; 140.6; Isa 26.7. 7 out of the -:8 are from the first part of Proverbs (cc. 1-9).

303   65.14; 73.6.

304   Qal 1:1 (5.13); Piel 3:1 (8.6; 65.12; 103.4); Hiphil 0:1.

305   9.12; 14.1; 66.5; 77.13; 78.11; 99.8; 103.7; 105.1; 141.4; 1 Sam 2.3. Prose (עֲלִילֹתֶ֫יהָ) Jer 32.19. Of the -:12, two thirds are from Ezekiel, partly from passages which are almost identical. Cf. No. 97.

306   25.6; 41.14; 90.2; 93.2; 103.17; 119.52; Isa 63.16, 19; 64.3. Prose Ne 9.5; 1 Ch 29.10. Cf. Nos. 98-101.

307   74.1; 80.5; 104.32; 144.5.

308   6.8; 31.10 f. Partial identity of 6.8 and 31.10.

309   53.6; 89.11; 112.9; 141.7; 147.16.

310   136.24; Lam 5.8. Qal, all meanings, 3:1 (7.3).

311   Sing. 25/24+4 prose:30 (9.10; 10.1; 20.2; 22.12; 37.39; 50.15; 54.9; 77.3; 78.49; 81.8; 86.7; 91.15; 116.3; 120.1; 138.7; 142.3; 143.11; Isa 33.2; 63.9; Jer 14.8; 15.11; 16.19; Jonah 2.3; Na 1.7 [Hab 3.16; cf. n. 89]. Prose 2 Ki 19.3; Ne 9.27, 37; 2 Ch 20.9). Pl. 7:6 (25.17, 22; 31.8; 34.7, 18; 46.2; 71.20).

312   35.14; 38.7; 42.10.

313   26.12; 68.27.

314   74.1; 79.13; 95.7; 100.3.

315   139.2, 17.

316   94.19; 139.23.

317   20.6; 37.4.

318   18.12; 36.6; 57.11; 68.35; 77.18; 78.23; 89.7, 38.

319   Job 10.24; 38.11 are not counted; meaning
uncertain.

320   Verb 2:0 (119.40, 174).   תָּאְבָה 119.20.   All from
one psalm.

321   61.3.

322   <u>Piel</u> and <u>Pual</u> do not occur.

323   25.21; 119.7.   Prose 1 Ch 29.17b.   (But is this
half verse really part of the prayer and not rather a mere
account?   Note that the first half verse, which is certainly
part of the prayer 29.10 ff., has 79) מִישָׁרִים!).

324   46.10; 61.3; 135.7.

325   72.4; 94.5; 143.3 (דִּכָּא); (89.11 [תִּדַּכְּאֵם mss.; var.
תְּדַכֶּה]).   Note that in the last two occurrences the vocalization
is that of דכה, with one variant even spelled as a ל״ה verb.
The Masoretes contributed their pointing, or, more likely,
had a reliable tradition to make the dichotomy: psalms דכה -
outside דכא almost perfect.

326   33.17; 41.2; 89.49; 107.20; 116.4.

327   33.3; 68.26; Isa 38.20.

328   Pp. 64 f.

329   Jer 12.1b, part of Jeremiah's "Confessions", can

hardly be counted among prayers. It is the question that
opens discussion and argument.

330   18.2, probably a later addition, not in 2 Sam 22.
Read פֶּרֶץ Isa 40.10 with 1QIs^a.

331   68.36; Job 30.21.

332   Of little importance for this study are: אֹפֶק (פ)
(0:3), an Aramaic loan (GB, p. 888) in Esther and Daniel;
אֹמֶן (ן), אַמְצָה, מַאֲמַצִּים (each one 0:1; 1QIs^a Isa 40.26 has וְאַמִּיץ
כֹּחוֹ [for MT כֹּחַ וְאַמִּיץ] which is certainly אַמִּיץ כֹּחוֹ as in LXX);
rare, late (?).   חַיִל covers a wide range of meanings, and it is
often difficult to say where "power, might" ends and others
begin.

333   47.9.

334   The exceptions are: Jer 19.19-23; Ps 133;
Lam 3.43-45 (these two have three verses each) and some psalm
splinters of one or two verses.

335   In order to assure a rather equal number of
printed words per page, the following procedure was adopted:
Items of psalm language were counted on the first 23 pages
of the Book of Psalms in the Letteris Bible in so far as
the pages are fully printed (this excludes, for example,
the first page [p. 991]) and contain the beginnings of two
chapters (this excludes, for example, pp. 992 and 995).
The following chart gives the result of the counting.

Page	993	994	1002	1005	1010	1012	1017
Words per page	24	23	31	14	15	9	27

Page	1020	1022	1023	1025	1026	1027
Words per page	14	14	15	22	19	27

Page	1028	1029	1030	1038	1043	1044
Words per page	25	17	21	17	15	12

Page	1045	1046	1050	1051
Words per page	21	18	31	28

336   GuBe. For this investigation, I accepted not only
Gunkel's concept and system as a whole (yet cf. p. 35 and
n. 338), but also his classification of the individual psalms.
Although I differ with Gunkel about some details of the classification, it would be out of place to argue the point of a few
minor differences, the net result of which would not affect the
picture to any appreciable extent. In order to follow Gunkel
closely, this survey is limited to the poems of the Book of
Psalms. Part of the psalms contained in other biblical books
are mentioned in GuBe but not utilized for the study of the
Gattungen as completely as those of the Psalter which have the
benefit of the full interpretation in GuPs.

337) 71) חסד 98(!)+12 prose:84 is omitted.

338   Liturgies are broken up where feasible and their
parts classified under their respective Gattungen. "Oracles"
(retaining Gunkel's ill fitting term), i.e. voicings of reve-
lations, which are often parts of liturgies, are set apart here
and constitute a Gattung of their own. Likewise, large subunits
of a single psalm, which belong to a Gattung other than the
psalm itself, are classified under their own Gattung. Example:
Ps 22 as a whole is a lamentation of an individual. Vv. 23-32
are the thanksgiving song which the psalmist will sing at his

future salvation; they are entered here as a thanksgiving song. Often classification is difficult, sometimes impossible, as in the case of Ps 119.

339   It is clear from the preceding note that the figures of this column can have no more than an approximate value.

340   GuBe, pp. 254-256.

341   This term is borrowed by the research of linguistic types from that of literary types where it was introduced by Gunkel.

342   Recent contributions to this question are G. von Rad; E. Würthwein, both in *Festschrift A. Bertholet*, 1950, pp. 418-437 and 532-549, respectively; S. Mowinckel, HUCA 23, I (1950-51), pp. 205-231. All three lean toward the cultic (guild) view.

343   Jer 11.18-20 (12.1-3); 15.11, 15-18; 16.19; 17.14-18; 18.19-23; 20.7-13.

344   The similarities in Ps 31 seem to depend on Jeremiah.

345   This has been shown by Y. Kaufmann, *Toledot ha'emuna hayisre'elit* II, 1944 f., pp. 701 f. and *passim*.

346   Jer 20.13. The authenticity of this verse has been denied by the following scholars on the ground of its similarity with the psalms: B. Duhm, *Das Buch Jeremia*, 1901, p. 166; P. Volz, *Der Prophet Jeremia*, 1922, p. 209, n. 1; S.H. Blank, *Introduction and Critical Notes to...Jeremiah...*,

1940-41, p. 42 (mimeographed). Others have maintained it:
F. Giesebrecht, Das Buch Jeremia, 1894, p. 114; A.W. Streane,
Jeremiah, 1903, p. 148; S.R. Driver, The Book of the Prophet
Jeremiah, 1906, p. 119; L.E. Binns, The Book of the Prophet
Jeremiah, 1919, p. 158; W. Rothstein in E. Kautzsch[4] - A. Bertholet, Die Heilige Schrift des AT I, 1922, p. 782, n. d;
Y. Kaufmann, l. c.; W. Rudolph, Jeremia, 1947, p. 115. Since
the "Confessions" as a whole, whose authenticity is not ques-
tioned, exhibit the closest relationship to the psalms in style
and thought, one should not make this similarity a means of
higher criticism. Volz arrives with his method at distant
terminals: "Der אביון ist der geistlich Arme der Psalmensprache."
The poor in spirit, however, do not pertain to allegedly late
psalms but to Mat 5.3.

347   Jer 32.6 ff.

348   Jer 26.17 ff., 24; 36.11 ff.; 37.3; 38.7 ff.,
14 ff.

349   17.14.

350   15.18.

351   Cf. the list in H. Schmidt, Die Psalmen, 1934,
p. VI, which can be amplified.

352   Modern scholars and readers of the Bible tend
to consider the prophets as innovators venturing into hitherto
unknown realms of religious experience. Nothing was farther
from the prophets' own consciousness. All they professed to
do was to preserve the old, which was good, as opposed to the

new, which was bad. Only rarely did they speak of something
altogether new (e.g. Jer 31.31 ff.) and then, too, in the name
of the old.

353   Outside of prayers, the diction of the poetic
addresses of the prophets does not seem to have anything in
common with psalm language. The linguistic approach does
not favor recent hypotheses of cult prophets in Israel and
their traceability in the Bible.

354   The turn the preceding chapter took toward its
end does not militate against this. Though figures played
no role there, the approach was nevertheless quantitative:
the extension of the use of psalm language was investigated
there.

355   The reader might occasionally prefer a different
arrangement of the material within the groups as well as a
different distribution of the material among these groups.
Such different arrangement would not affect the course and
the outcome of this part of the study. An item is also entered
into one of the groups if almost all its occurrences belong
to it. Thus 79) מישרים is listed in the first group, third
paragraph, although among its 8(+1 prose) occurrences there
are 2 (58.2; Isa 26.7; and 1 prose [1 Ch 29.17]) which do not
refer to God.

356   The pious are joyous at God's salvation.

357   Here subgrouping is only approximate.

358   Some formations which were presented in the above

list for the sake of completeness and comparison, e.g.
No. 140 b), are not considered here.

359   Nine words or word groups are not included in the
preceding lists   although they belong to them conceptually:
1) אנף Qal (as against Hitpael); 67) חיה Piel (as against
Hiphil); 129) מַשְׂנִא (as against שׂנוא). It is not the idea
of giving or restoring life, conveyed by חיה, nor that of
anger, expressed by אנף ; it is rather the Piel and the Qal
whose meanings are identical with those of the Hiphil and the
Hitpael, respectively, that are peculiar to the psalms.
Similarly, one could hardly maintain that the psalmists had
the categories of singularity or plurality in mind when using
42) תך in the sing. instead of the pl., and 36) מרמה;
133) משכן ; 135) תהום in the pl. and not in the sing. which
is common otherwise.   In the case of 136)$\sqrt{ישׁע}$ and 137) I$\sqrt{עזז}$,
it is not the overall frequency of these roots but the particular derivations from them as well as their use in certain
phrases which constitute psalm language.

360   See n. 162.

361   144.12 uses הֵיכָל in a purely architectural sense
referring to a fine building and not necessarily the Temple
in Jerusalem.   The ratio for הֵיכָלְךָ is 3:0, for הֵיכְלוֹ 3:3.

362   N. 15 imposes some restraint on this conclusion.

363   Cf. GB, p. 1009, s.v. "Wunder", but what he notes
as the fourth word, מופת, does not belong there.   LVT, pp. 504 f.
is certainly correct in not translating מופת by "Wunder" as GB,

p. 407, does but by "Wahrzeichen", "sign, token". It is not an item of psalm language (4+1 prose:26)!

364 See n. 44.

365 Bab. Sanhedrin 106b.

366 There is nothing to substantiate H.J. Stoebe's statement to the contrary (VT 2 [1952], p. 254). The passages which he quotes in nn. 1-3 indicate, if anything, the active meaning of חָמִיד (for Dt 33.8 cf. above, n. 106), as one can also gather from some aspects which he develops from the word חֶמֶד.

367 See n. 106.

368 The opposing views are most clearly brought forth by A. Goetze, Language 17 (1941), pp. 127-138, (non-Canaanite) and W.F. Albright, BASOR 89 (1943), pp. 7 f., (Canaanite). Recent contributions are J. Cantineau, Semitica 3 (1950), pp. 21-34, with partial bibliography, and N.H. Tur-Sinai, Tarbiz 23 (1951 f.), pp. 143-145.

369 L. Bloomfield, Language, 1933, pp. 317 f.; Z.S. Harris, Development of the Canaanite Dialects (Am. Or. Ser. 16), 1939 , pp. 16, 91; A. Goetze, Language 17 (1941), p. 168. The wave theory as such is by no means a new concept in linguistics; it goes back to J. Schmidt who expounded it as early as 1872 (cf. Bloomfield, l.c.).

370 Cultural influence on Israel by Phenicia has been assumed for the seventh to the second centuries B.C. At that time, it has been ascertained, concepts known from Ugarit,

found their way into Israel (W.F. Albright, From the Stone Age to Christianity, 1940, pp. 243 f.). This theory does not concern our deliberations, since it does not explain the linguistic affinities (to be presented here) between the psalms on the one hand, and Phenician and Ugaritic on the other hand. These linguistic affinities are found in all kinds of psalms, including the simplest ones which do not exhibit the faintest traces of Canaanite myths, similes, etc. Conversely, conceptual and purely literary elements are rather easily transferable, without thereby affecting the language of the absorbing literature. Inasmuch as the impact on the biblical psalms of a civilization at present attested to only in the literature from Ugarit is said to have been felt since the seventh century, it must be completely divorced from the Ugaritic language which, by that time, had been a dead language for many centuries and was certainly no longer understood by the Israelites.

371   The glossary of Sl. is quoted by page numbers. Figures, not preceded by p(age), refer to the numbers of the inscriptions.

372   Cf. n. 34.

373   The dialect of this inscription of the King of Ḥamath and Laᶜash contains elements known from Phenician and Aramaic texts, respectively, with the Phenician component slightly dominant; cf. M. Lidzbarski, Ephemeris für semitische Epigraphik III, 1909-1915, p. 2, and J.A. Montgomery, JBL 28 (1909), p. 64. For the problem of its classification cf. the

remarks about Northwest Semitic dialects, p. 52 and
n. 433

374   This word is usually explained by (Montgomery,
l.c., p. 69: "must[!] be connected with") the Ar. عَدّ , "count"
and translated "astrologers" or similarly. But the Late
Babylonian passage which Montgomery adduces for comparison
is hardly a parallel. In the first place, the correctness of
his interpretation of Akk. tupšar mināti, on which his explanation rests, is questionable; cf. B. Meissner, Babylonien
und Assyrien II, 1925, p. 380. Secondly, what holds true for
the highly developed and sophisticated civilization of Nabo-
nidus, may not be so in an outlying little kingdom of Northern
Syria. Astrology was apparently regarded by foreigners as
something typically Babylonian (Isa 47.13). The essence of
the message of the seers and עדן is preserved in lines 13-15.
It is a message of hope and moral support. What the עדן ,
then, do for the king is עדד in the sense of the psalms,
bolster his morale. They appear together with the חזין , as
does in the same function the מבשר together with the צפים
in Isa 52.7 f. (cmp. 40.9). (With the discovery of the inscriptions from Ugarit, עדד has been interpreted as "messengers"
on the basis of ʿdd [UH 51:VII:46] which, in turn, is said to
mean just this on the basis of its supposed parallel dll and
the latter's alleged meaning "leader" [line 45]; cf. H.L. Ginsberg, Ketave ʾugarit (The Ugarit Texts), 1936, p. 40. But
everything is uncertain; cf. C.H. Gordon, Ugaritic Literature,

1949, p. 36. In the meantime, Ginsberg has given up the basis of his exegesis [in Ancient Near Eastern Texts Relating to the O.T., ed. J.B. Pritchard, 1950, p. 135a] and apparently connects it now with Akk. dalālu, "serve". A relation of ʿdd with tʿdt [// mlảk, UH 137:22, 26, 30 (41, 44)] is likewise questionable; it is implicitly denied UH § 18.1457 and § 18.1466.)

375   Har., p. 131. The one occurrence of ז‎y outside of nomm. pr. is that in a bilingual inscription from Lapethos, Cyprus: ‎ם‎ʼ‎ה ז‎y ‎נ‎ז‎y‎ʼ where the Greek text Ἀθηνᾷ Σωτείρᾳ Νίκῃ favors the derivation from √‎ז‎ʼ‎ז‎y. For ז‎ŷ in the sense of "victory" see W.F. Albright, HUCA 23, I (1950-51), p. 31. But we must not build too much on literalism in such trans-lations. In nomm. pr. a decision is impossible in most cases.

376   There is nothing unusual in encountering this pl. frequently in a language recording polytheistic texts. See the long list of references Sl., p. 354, and noté also the El-Amarna n. pr. Bin-Elīm, "Son of the god(s)" (EA 256.15; cf. W.F. Albright, BASOR 89 [1943], p. 11, n. 25) and the refer-ences below. What is remarkable is the possibility that linguistic traces of an older religion are best discernible in the psalms. On the other hand, it must be borne in mind that the pl. of ʼil fairly often denotes one god in Syria-Palestine. 1) In Ugarit the god Ktr-wḤss is spoken of as ilm; this form governs the pl. of the accusative pronoun hmt (2 Aqht:V:20, 29 f.). T.H. Gaster, Thespis, 1950, p. 281,

explains these passages otherwise, obviously in order to
avoid the pl. of the form for the sing. of the object. Such
caution is unnecessary, for there are similar constructions
2) in the El-Amarna letters where the Egyptian king is addressed
as ilānūia, "my gods" (EA 283.2) and the pl. ilānu is con-
structed with the sing. of the verb(s) liš'al (96.4 ff.)
and perhaps ellak (189. rev 13 f.; this form, however, may
be a Canaanitism in that the verb, which precedes the subject,
might be used in the sing. regardless of the grammatical number
of its subject). Finally, confirmation is found in 3) Phenician,
cf. Har. pp. 60, 77. Looking over this material, one is no
longer sure whether אלים,   בני אלים (Ps 29.1; 89.7) mean a
sing. or a pl. Cf. also R. Kittel, Die Psalmen, 5th and 6th
ed., 1929, p. 110.

377   Frdr § 249, 1.

378   Sl., p. 369.

379   Har., p. 101 f.; ZKR 1.14 with metathesis חצל.

380   yi-iḫ-na-nu-ni; ye-en-ni-nu-nu-mi, "he is gracious
to me/us" (EA 137.81; 253.24 [the last -mi is Akkadian].
In both cases the subject is the Pharao. An occasional tinge
of deification belongs to the [pseudo-] feudal style of the
El-Amarna correspondence); Sl. 233.4 (correctly translated here
but wrongly entered in the glossary, p. 362, as n. pr.);
possibly Sl. 277.5 (cf. Sl.'s remark, a.l.).

381   Relatively much more frequent than corresponding
Hebrew names; cf. Har., p. 103.

382   The main source for עליון in the Canaanite realm
is Sanchunyathon in Eusebius, Praep. Evang., I:10:14. - The
name is further represented in the n. pr. Πυγμαλίων
Hüsing, quoted by Türk in W.H. Roscher, Ausführliches Lexicon
der griechischen und römischen Mythologie III (1897-1909),
col. 3318, explains it as Pumay (= פמי), "als ʿeljon עליון
(= geljon) bezeichnet." Phonetically much simpler is Sl.'s
way (pp. 199 f.), but his interpretation needs correction.
The meaning of Πυγμαλίων , then, is: "Puʿm is (the god) Elyon,"
or simply:"Puʿm is the Most High." For Puʿm cf. Har., p. 138,
(II פעם). (The name Πυγμαλίων ascertains the u-vowel of the
divine name II פעם [against du Mesnil du Buisson, Mélanges
Syriens...R. Dussaud I, p. 424] and separates it phonetically
from I פעם, "foot", whose vowel is a or i, according to both
Heb. פעם and Akk. pēnu, or just a, if we are to follow Frdr.
§ 75 a in explaining the Punic n. pr. Namp(h)amo as "'Güte'
und 'Fuss'".) - עליון in the Phenician orbit is further attested to by the Sidonian n. pr. Abdolonymos,i.e., in Hebrew
spelling, עבד-עליונים; cf. G. Kuhn, ZAW 57 (1939), p. 150.
עליונים is pl. in form and sing. in meaning; cf. above, n. 376,
and GK § 124 h, i. - For the presence of עליון among other
Semitic groups cf. G.L. Della Vida, JBL 63 (1944), pp. 2 f.,
nn. 6 f.; for עליון (אל) in general cf. especially J. Lewy,
RHR 110 (1934), pp. 50-65, and H.S. Nyberg, ARW 35 (1938),
pp. 343, 350 ff., passim. For the corresponding form in Ugarit
cf. p. 50.

383 Six in Sl., p. 371,(read the third reference 22.8!) and one Azitawadda, lion, 2.

384 Cmp. the <u>n. pr.</u> פלסבעל whose first component Har., p. 137, explains as <u>Piel</u>. This interpretation is possible,in view of the verb form in the Heb. name יְפַלֵּט (1 Ch 7.32 f., cmp. Jos 16.3), but not cogent,in view of the substantive in the Hebrew names אֱלִיפֶלֶט and פַּלְטִיאֵל.

385 Sl., pp. 372 f.; Har., p. 138.

386 Har., p. 138. Two names, פעלאבסת and פעלעשתרת, are composed of a substantive, corresponding to Heb. פֹּעַל, or the verb and a divine name; two others, אלפעל and יאלפעל, containing the verb, express the same idea. The doubtful קרפעל is not counted.

387 Sl. 22.7; 129.4 (with repetitions in lines 6, 8, 10). All other references given by Sl., p. 373, have either other meanings or have not been explained satisfactorily.

388 <u>pa-né-mu</u> (EA 155.46), that is <u>panēmo</u>; <u>ta-ah-ta-mu</u> (EA 252.26), that is <u>tahtāmo</u>; <u>ma-ah-sé-ra-mu</u> (EA 287.16), that is <u>mahserāmo</u> for biblical Heb. מַחְסוֹרָמוֹ; O. Schröder's normalization *<u>ma'aśiramo</u> for biblical Heb. מַעְשִׂירָמוֹ (OLZ 18 [1915], coll. 38 f.) is unlikely.

389 This is the form of the Old Byblos dialect (four occurrences there and one in Klmw II, Frdr. § 293). Written with ד (דחם), it also occurs in the Phen. incantation from Arslan Tash, <u>Mélanges Syriens...R.Dussaud</u> I, 1939, pp. 422 f., <u>tranche</u>.

390   This phrase, which is unique in the El-Amarna letters (generally in Akkadian the pronominal subject of a verbal sentence is not separately expressed), is part of, or precedes, a "Canaanite psalm fragment"; cf. n. 448. Like its Hebrew psalm counterpart it means: Formerly I thought or intended (but now I know that I was wrong).

391   This word for "throne" occurs in EA 120.18 as ka-aḫ-šu together with iršu "couch"; cf. UH § 18.962 (but not a "gloss"). According to J. Friedrich, ZDMG 96 (1942), p. 491, it is derived from Ḫur. kišhi.

392   UH 76:III:14 f.

393   49:I:30 f.

394   68:9; 3 Aqht:(obv.)38; ʿnt:II:8.

395   ilm occurs frequently; some references UH § 18.119. Cf. also n. 376.

396   49:II:18 f.

397   51:VII:51 f.

398   The first four references of UH § 18.385, with, perhaps, some of the following ones to be added. See the discussion there.

399   125:15.

400   Krt:91 infinitive (nomen actionis).

401   The signs for the verbal stems are those of UH § 9.28.

402   2 Aqht:VI:32 f.

403   1 Aqht:15 f.

133

404   51:IV:48 (= ᶜnt:V:44) with El as subject.

405   Nyberg has shown (l. c. [n. 382], p. 343, that עליון is a later lengthening of ᶜAly. The Ugaritic passage quoted here, which was published after he had written his article, nicely confirms what he says about ᶜAly/ᶜAlw on pp. 344 f.

406   126:III:5 f. (7 f.). The translation is H.L. Ginsberg's, The Legend of King Keret (BASOR, Supplem. Stud. 2 f.), 1946, p. 29.

407   3 Aqht:(rev.?)13.

408   UH § 18.1656; not exhaustive.

409   mṣlt (75:II:62) // ᶜn // qr, which are other words for subterranean water.

410   68:9; ᶜnt:III:34 (=IV:48=50). The constant parallel to ỉb, "enemy" makes the meaning, abstractum pro concreto, certain.

411   qm.aḫk, "thy brother's foe(s)" (75:II:25) // ỉby, "mine enem(y/ies)".

412   51:V:65. The translation is Gaster's, Thespis, 1950, pp. 173, 447.

413   According to UH § 13.16, lmšknth (2 Aqht:V:32 f.) is"probably" pl. in form but to be translated as sing. "to his residence". This is the case with other words for dwellings, "unmistakably" with bht (pl. cstr.), "house" (e.g. 129:8; ᶜnt:II:4) and possibly with hklm in various passages (cf. UH § 18.593).

414   49:I:6 (=51:IV:22=2 Aqht:VI:48); 1 Aqht:45.
thm[   ] (52:30 f.) may be the remainder of the dual. thmt
(2 Aqht:VI:12) is not clear; pl. (?).

415   UH § 6.38-41.

416   ʿnt:II:23; possibly Krt:22 f. mid follows the
modified word 54:13 and apparently 55:27. Note that the 1/2
cases with preceding mid are from epics and thus represent a
somewhat older stage in the development of Ugaritic, while
the passages with the inverse order are from a letter and a
hippiatric prescription, respectively, and seem to reflect
a younger phase of the language. If conclusions on this
narrow basis are permitted, it would seem that Ugaritic and
Hebrew were exposed to the same trend of postponing certain
adverbs. (In 51:V:77 [=94=100]; 95:11 f., mid has nominal
function rather than adverbial as in the other Ugaritic passages
and in those from the psalms, quoted in n. 259).

417   51:V:113-116.

418   2 Aqht:VI:28 f. My attention to these Ugaritic
passages has been attracted by M.D. (U.) Cassuto, Haʾela ʿanat
(The Goddess Anath), 1951, p. 38. The second passage is slightly
different from the biblical examples of No. 166 in that the
sequence is not transitive-intransitive but doubly transitive-
simply transitive stems.

419   See the references in Albright's article, l. c.
(n. 266).

420   Th. Bauer, Die Ostkanaanäer, 1926, p. 42. Both

names are from Chiera's list (cf. pp. 3-5).

421   ARM I, 39.19'; II, 10.7'.

422   M. Noth, in <u>Geschichte und AT, A. Alt...darge-</u>
<u>bracht</u>, 1953, p. 141, counts <u>nomm. pr.</u> of this type among
characteristically West Semitic names.

423   ARM V, p. 123, from an unpublished text
(G. Dossin). - The exact Hebrew correspondent, עֲזֶנֶג, belonging
to the vocabulary of the <u>Piyutim</u>, does not appear before the
Middle-Ages.

424   ARM V, 35-45, lines 3. - Ch. Jean,in <u>Studia</u>
<u>Mariana</u>, 1950, p. 81, considers a Hurrian etymology as an
alternative!

425   Cf. M. Lidzbarski, <u>Ephemeris</u>...II, 1908, pp. 18 f.

426   References from five documents are listed by
Jean, <u>l. c.</u> (n. 424), p. 97. For the god Hammu see J. Lewy,
HUCA 18 (1944), pp. 429-488.

427   Name of several persons, Bauer, <u>l. c.</u> (n. 420),
p. 42. This onomastic type is quite common among Akkadian
names: $\check{S}u/\check{S}a(t)-^{d}N$. It makes no substantial difference
that in the examples of No. 157 full clauses are subordinated
to the pronouns and in the name Zū-Ilā it is a substantive.
In both cases, zū etc. is cstr. which governs either a genitive
clause or a nominal genitive. The determinative pronoun,
governing a nominal genitive, occurs in Hebrew in the psalm
passage Ju 5.5 (=Ps 68.9): זֶה סִינַי, "He of Sinai"; bibliography
LVT, p. 251.

428   In view of the fact that part of the Phenician
and all of the "Amorite" comparative material has been drawn
from personal names, it might be asked why early biblical
nomm. pr. have not been admitted to this study for the same
purpose. Noth, l. c. (n. 422), pp. 142-149, has demonstrated
that certain groups of Hebrew names are probably of great
antiquity. The inclusion of biblical names here, however, is
not recommended. The course of the investigation would lead
over treacherous ground, since the line between old and young
biblical nomm. pr. cannot always be drawn with certainty.
Again, possible damage to method deserves more attention than
possible gains in substance.

429   It goes without saying that - to my knowledge -
the words listed above are not found in Akkadian proper, i.e.
Akkadian as spoken by people without a Northwest Semitic background.

430   I can infer nothing else from the material and
the discussion in M. Noth's article ZA 39 (1929 f.), pp. 213 ff.,
especially pp. 217-219.

431   Hommel's early attempts to emphasize (South)
Arabic relationship have been refuted by Bauer, l. c. (n. 420),
pp. 69 f., as have P. Dhorme's interposing considerations (RB
37 [1928], pp. 164 f.), again by Bauer in ZA 38 (1928 f.),
pp. 154-160, 166-168. I shall, therefore, discuss only those
points of Dhorme's argumentation (and in Dhorme's order) which
Bauer passed over. 1) The final -ā in -ilā does not point to

Arab. اَلِ (why not to Heb. or Aram. אלה ?), but is the same
vowel as in the Aramaic determ. state; cf. J. Lewy (five
references in Jean, l.c. [n. 424], p. 71, n. 33); I.J. Gelb,
Old Akkadian Writing and Grammar (Mater. for the Assyr. Dictionary 2), 1952, p. 196; M. Birot, RA 47 (1953), p. 129; as an
example see the above mentioned n. pr. Ṣūrā-Ḥammū. 2) The component
ʿamm is so frequent in the biblical onomasticon that it is
hard to see how it can be adduced to prove anything for the
alleged (South) Arabic element. 3) The word ba-al has
nothing to do with Arab. خَال, "maternal uncle", but, as Nyberg
has taught us (l. c.[n. 382], pp. 330 ff.), stands for the
divine name ʿal. 4) That the spelling SA-am-SU etc. in nomm. pr.,
containing the name of the sun-god, cannot be quoted as evidence for an Arabic background of those nomm. pr., has been
shown by Bauer and can now be even better substantiated on the
elaborate basis of Gelb's investigation, l. c., pp. 48 ff.
It must be stated against Bauer, however, that this orthography
is not indicative of the actual pronunciation of the sibilant
š₁ and š₃ (Gelb's numbering). In ancient as well as in modern
personal names, spellings are often retained which have been
discarded in general writing. Thus Old Assyrian writing represents a modernization and simplification with respect to earlier
and contemporary stages of Akkadian writing. But in names
of people and gods it makes occasional use of syllabic signs
and values, otherwise discontinued or extremely rare, such as
ṣi in ṭāb-ṣi-lá-a-šùr (Textes Cunéiformes, Musée du Louvre XX ,

173.5); úr in nu-úr-ki-li (l. c., 178.14), nu-úr-ištar (Inscriptions Cunéiformes du Kultépé I, 1952, 6.17); i in (-)i-li(-)(passim, as at all times); ši as complement in šamši^{ši} (passim); šùr(=ŠIR)in a-šùr (passim; the spelling probably reflects an older pronunciation Ašir, cmp. the name of his parhedros אֲשֵׁרָה and J. Lewy's detailed argumentation l. c. [n. 426], pp. 461 f.). It is unlikely that the peculiar orthography of Northwest Semitic names represents a set of foreign phonemes, retained within the Old Babylonian dialect for the pronunciation of those names, as it is true that non-English phonemes in modern United States surnames of foreign extraction have disappeared despite the retention of their foreign orthography. Positively speaking, the dialect of the Northwest Semitic names represents, in general, a stage of linguistic development not later than the end of the Old Akkadian period (ca. 1950 B.C.), with an earlier time more likely. - 5) With regard to the rest of the supposedly (South) Arabic names the following remarks will suffice (the length of the i, postulated by Dhorme, is nowhere indicated in the originals): compare Aminum with אֲמִינוֹן (2 Sa 13.20); Ḥazizum with עֲזִיזָא (Ezra 10.27; yet Ḥazizum, and perhaps also עֲזִיזָא, may be Akkadian [cf. LVT, p. 695, s. v.עֲזִיזָא]; or else the first name may be normalized ḫa-sí-sú-um, an abbreviated name, cmp. marduk-ḫa-si-is [H. Ranke, Early Babylonian Personal Names, 1905, p. 121]). Sapirum means "governor", as does סֹפֵר (Ju 5.14; cf. my note, HUCA 24 [1952 f.], p. 107. An Akkadian name of similar meaning is Sukallia). Ṣabium is probably Akkadian (Bauer, ZA

38, p. 168), but a Hebrew etymology is possible in view of the
fem. name צביה (2 Ki 12.2). There remains only one name which
points clearly to (South) Arabic, Ḥalilum.

432   Cf. Cantineau, l. c. (n. 368), p. 34, following
Goetze.

433   Cf. also F. Rosenthal, JAOS 72 (1952), pp. 171 f.

434   Pp. 30 f.

435   It must, however, be noted that, in the case of
q) (No. 17),   Klmw I, 9 has ישבה.על.כסא.אבי.

436   G. Bergsträsser's suspicion of these stems
(Hebräische Grammatik II, 1929, § 20 b) is gratuitous. Likewise, it is questionable whether one can maintain the separation of the Poel etc. of the strong verbs from that of the
y″y (and ע″וי) verbs, even in the cautious formulation of
H. Bauer-P. Leander, Historische Grammatik..., 1922, § 38 k.
It seems preferable to explain the forms סובֵב etc. as a natural
selection on the part of the mediae geminatae between the first
and the second sets in order to avoid the triplication of the
second radical.

437   Cmp. Bauer-Leander, §§ 56 l', 58 x. The beginnings of this trend are barely perceptible in classical Hebrew,
but in Middle Hebrew it has become predominant; cf. M.Ṣ. Segal,
Diqduq leshon hamishna, 1935 f., pp. 144 f., 148 f. Observe
that also with respect to No. 136A) ישועה, an item of psalm
language, as compared with תשועה, which is not psalm language
(cf. n. 189), the line of the historic development is clearly:

psalm language, common biblical Hebrew, Middle Hebrew.

438   It occurs in the Song of Deborah (Ju 5.28).

439   It is found 72 times in the Bible.

440   Disregarding those listed in n. 332 for reasons given there.

441   dq.ảnm (UH 49:I:22) is sometimes connected with Heb. (אַדִּיק and) אוֹנִים (T.H. Gaster, Thespis, 1950, p. 449; Ginsberg, l. c.[n. 374], p. 140, doubtingly). It is a good guess, not generally accepted (cf. C.H. Gordon, Ugaritic Literature, 1949, p. 44), and awaits confirmation and linguistic usability.

442   This root has other meanings in the cognate languages. With the meaning peculiar to Hebrew, it occurs only in the Aramaic of the Babylonian Talmud, and there only once (according to the dictionaries) and as a verb(!) with the meaning "be strong" (Gittin 62a); the meaning is apparently an adaptation of the Aramaic idiom to the Hebrew language of law of the Mishnah under discussion which uses the same verb. J. Levy's translation (Chaldäisches Wörterbuch, 1867, p. 247) of מחפק באסטינ׳, "befestigt mit Stricken" (Targum Yerushalmi to Gen 50.1) is patently wrong. It must be "wrapped round with" as the variant shows: מחפק באסג׳ בוצא וארגמא, "wrapped with cloths of byssus and purple". (In view of this variant, should not אסטינ׳ here, contrary to its usual meaning "rope", mean "linen" as Heb. אטון and Greek ὀθόνη ?)

443   Also here, Jewish Aramaic, which alone, besides

Hebrew, has this word, is no proof of its genuine Aramaism.
It is either the untranslated Hebrew word that we find in the
Targum, or it is part of the Babylonian Talmudic formula
כח דהיתרא עדיף (ליה) , "(showing) the power of the more lenient
opinion is preferred," which recurs eight times. (Cf. Masoret
Hashas to Bab. Berakhot 60a. One reference is incorrectly
given there and has not been verified.) Both the restriction
of כח to this formula, usually following a sentence like
להודיעך כחו דר' פלוני, "to show the power of Rabbi N," as well
as the lack of the final Aleph leave little doubt that Aramaic
has borrowed it from Hebrew.

444   To the speaker or the writer, who chooses his
words, it does not matter whether the innovation is an
etymological or only a semantical one. חזק and all those
other words were "Modern Hebrew" in their day.

445   The alternatives depend on the counting or not
counting of Nos. 63, 105, 107, 133 and the double or simple
counting of עז Nos. 27 and/or 94.

446   See the preceding note.

447   Among such parallels are: 168) אל (81 [79]+6 prose:
126/127) - Sl. p. 354, UH § 18.119; 178) לדור דור...(19/18:
23/24) - UH § 18.561; 190) כבד..., "organ of thinking and
feeling" (4:2) - UH § 18.946; 193) מחץ verb (5/4:7/8) -
UH § 18.1161; 198) נעים (5/6:6/7) - Sl., p. 368; רָקָרָק חָרוּץ
(hap. leg., 68.14) - UH § 18.922; and others.

448   Cf. n. 5. - The so called "Canaanite psalm fragments"

of the El-Amarna letters are, of course, no exception. The
most comprehensive and indeed convincing presentation of the
case is that of A. Jirku, JBL 52 (1933), pp. 108-120, where
earlier literature is mentioned in nn. 1-4. Unfortunately,
the "Canaanite" psalms are preserved in (barbarian) Akkadian.

449   HUCA 23, I (1950-51), p. 3.

449a   Translators of the Hebrew Bible into modern
languages, trying to convey form as well as content of the
original, may want to take into consideration the archaic
character of psalm language. Their translation of the psalms
will be distinguished by a more archaic, "prayer book" flavor
of its language than that of the rest of the Bible.

450   ZA 40 (1932), pp. 163-227; 41 (1933), pp. 90-183,
236. - Von Soden's study has come under attack by A. Poebel,
Studies in Akkadian Grammar (Assyr. Stud. [Chicago], No.9),
1939, pp. 69-74. This writer has not been convinced by the
gist of Poebel's arguments.

451   The comparison of the language of the biblical
psalms with the hymnic-epic dialect requires a few words of
comment. It has been said above, p. 13, that the student of
psalm language does not expect to find its main characteristics
in morphology. On the other hand, von Soden's inquiry is
chiefly based on morphological phenomena. Yet this method-
ological difference, rather than discrediting the approach of
either study, genuinely reflects the different functions and
fates of the two species of literature. For it has become

apparent that, among the sources of the hymnic-epic dialect, Enuma Elish, the Epic of Creation, shares only part of the morphological peculiarities of that dialect. This epic, known from numerous first millennium copies, has undergone a process of conscious and/or unconscious modernization on the part of the copyists and priests (ZA 40, p. 165, n. 1; 41, p. 180). It played a continuous and persistent role in the rites of the New Year festival at different sanctuaries, and it is small wonder that this constant usage made itself felt in the linguistic form, foremost in the grammar of the epic. Conversely, the majority of the rest of the poems that constitute our sources of that dialect have come down in Old Babylonian copies, up to twelve hundred years older than the extant Enuma Elish material, while the minority, the younger copies (and their Vorlagen), led a rather restful life in the libraries, where they were little exposed to the process of levelling certain morphological archaisms. The Hebrew psalms as a species and an unknown number of biblical psalms are comparable in function and fate to the Akkadian Enuma Elish. It is also for this reason that their grammar is less characteristic than their vocabulary.

452   Birnbaum's handling of this subject (P. Birnbaum, Sefer Hashana...(The Amer. Jew. Year Book) 8 f. (1946), pp. 330-353) is disappointing in spite of useful details, pp. 343-348. The periods of origin of the different prayers are not separated (p. 330). Expressions such a "lucidity of

style" (p. 348), instead of an analysis, tend to obscure things.

453   Cf. the brief remarks in A. Bendavid, <u>Leshon hamiqra' 'o leshon ḥakhamim</u>, 1950 f., pp. 161 f.

454   <u>Berakhot</u> 6.1.

455   I follow Albright in regarding Balaam's poems as among the very oldest pieces, originating from the early twelfth century B.C. (cf. JBL 63[1944], pp. 226-233; BASOR 118 [1950], p. 16, n. 13).

456   Quite recently, virtually the same contention has been made for the derivates of one root, viz. פעל (Nos. 106 f.; cf. p. 49). P. Humbert in ZAW 65, pp. 35-44 (issued August, 1953) has shown that the verb פעל and, to a lesser degree, its cognate substantives are heavily concentrated in the psalms, followed by wisdom literature, but rare in other parts of the Bible. Verb and, partly, substantives prominently signify Yhwh's gests with Israel. And particularly: Verb and substantives have probably been assimilated by the Hebrew language from Canaanite dialects.

457   It seems doubtful whether this alternative gets particular support by deriving the gentilic of that ancient sage, poet, and singer Ethan, viz. הָאֶזְרָחִי (1 Ki 5.11; Ps 89.1 [cmp. 88.1]), from אֶזְרָח, "aborigin" and then stating "that Hebrew temple music as such was recognized in Israel as going back to early pre-Israelite sources" (W.F. Albright, <u>Archeology and the Religion of Israel</u>, 1942, pp. 125-129; cf. also B. Maisler, <u>Bull. of the Jew. Pal. Expl. Soc.</u> 13 [1948 f.],

p. 107 [in Hebrew]). This etymology is countered by Chronicles,
(part of) LXX, and T, all of which interprete the gentilic as
descendant of Zarah, the son of Judah. Specifically, 1 Ch 2.6
deserves high regard as a piece of historical information or,
at least, as a witness of Israelite traditions, since the
Chronicler, always anxious to make prominent members of the
singer guilds descendants of Levi (1 Ch 6.16-32; 2 Ch 29.12-14
and elsewhere), does not touch their compromising pedigree
in this verse. - In a further argument along the same lines,
Albright suggests that the name כַּלְכֹּל (1 Ki 5.11; 1 Ch 2.6)
is identical with Kurkur, the name of a female singer from
Ascalon, probably from the thirteenth century B.C., mentioned
in an Egyptian source. While there is nothing linguistic
against this identification, it offers little substance for
historical inferences.

458   The discussion about the process of the settlement
of the Israelites in Palestine is irrelevant here. (The chief
exponents are A. Alt [PJ 35 (1939), pp. 8-63, republished in
Kleine Schriften zur Geschichte des Volkes Israel I, 1953,
pp. 126-174, particularly pp. 40 ff. and 153 ff., respectively]
on the one hand, and Y. Kaufmann [The Biblical Account of the
Conquest of Palestine, 1953, particularly pp. 86 ff.] on the
other hand. While Kaufmann maintains the correctness of the
account in the Book of Joshuah, viz. that the land was con-
quered and settled almost completely in Joshuah's days, it is
Alt's opinion that the settlement was a gradual and drawn-out

process which was not completed until a time considerably later than any date claimed for the Israelite immigration into that country.) For also within the general frame work of Alt's theory one is to postulate that the cultural contact of the Israelites with the indigenous population goes back to the very beginning of that process, and that the cultic influence of the Canaanites is as old as the establishment of Israelite sanctuaries on the soil of Palestine; cf. the technical term וַיֵּצֶב (Ju 8.27) and also the following passage, however hypothetical its formulation: תעבדון...את אלהי האמרי אשר אתם ישבים בארצם (Jos 24.15).

459   HUCA 23, I (1950-51), pp. 1 ff. H. Schmidt and T.H. Robinson preceded him in 1934 and 1939, respectively; see l. c., p. 9.

460   He assigns many individual songs, the beginnings of which are strung together in the catalogue, to the time from the thirteenth through the tenth centuries B.C. (l. c., pp. 9 f.); yet detailed datings are most difficult to ascertain.

461   1 Ch 15.16, 28; 16.5; 25.1, 6; 2 Ch 5.12; 20.28; 29.25. Also Ne 12.27. These and the following references are mainly from passages about the institution and regulations of the Temple service by David and Solomon. But it goes without saying that those few references from other legends reflect the cultic praxis of the time of the Chronicler no less faithfully than the majority. - It is not always possible to decide whether in a given case בכנורות,etc. is collective or pl.

in meaning. But it is easier than in the corresponding case
with 148) כנור; cf. n. 227. E.g. 2 Ch 9.11 is not entered
here, not only because it is not the Chronicler's own style
(cf. 1 Ki 10.12; occurrences from texts of other books which
are incorporated in Chronicles are not counted), but because
many single objects are meant and not a group of instruments
playing together. 1 Ch 25.3 has naturally the sing. for one
single instrument.

462   1 Ch 15.16, 20, 28; 16.5; 25.16; 2 Ch 5.12; 20.28;
29.25. Also Ne 12.27.

463   47.6; 81.4; 98.6; 150.3.

464   2 Ch 15.14. In Ne 4.12, 14 it is used for giving
signals outside of the Temple.

465   150.4. - From the absence of this instrument from
Chronicles, H. Gressmann, Musik und Musikinstrumente im AT,
1903, p. 29, infers that the psalms as a whole presuppose an
older era of Temple music than Chronicles does. GuPs, p. 623,
follows him, adding the fact that מינם is absent there, too.
This conclusion happens to coincide with that of the present
investigation. Yet the full burden of its proof is placed
on one (! or, GuPs, two) frail hap. leg.

466   150.5.

467   150.4.

468   1 Ch 13.8; 15.24, 28; 16.6, 42; 2 Ch 5.12; 20.28;
29.26, 27, 28. Also Ezra 3.10; Ne 12.35, 41. The word occurs
once in the psalms in the pl. (98.6), but the context (vv. 7 f.)

makes it clear that there the trumpets are no part of the
Temple music. By the same token, 2 Ch 15.14 is not counted
here.

469   1 Ch 13.8; 15.16, 19, 28; 16.5, 42; 25.1, 6;
2 Ch 5.12 f.; 29.25. Also Ezra 3.10; Ne 12.27.

470   Also amplified as כלי שיר יהוה/האלהים 1 Ch 15.16;
16.42; 2 Ch 5.13; 7.6; 23.13; 34.12.

471   2 Ch 29.26 f. Amplified כלי שיר דויד איש האלהים
Ne 12.36.

472   The word occurs at the beginning of the prayer
Ne 9.5-37. This prayer, incorporated in the work of the
Chronicler, is of Northern Israelite origin as A.C. Welch,
ZAW 47 (1929), pp. 135-137, has convincingly shown. I would
take exception only to Welch's early date, shortly after 722/21,
because of v. 32b: the time of the Assyrian empire belongs
to the past. Unless we assume a complete estrangement between
the Northern and the Southern territories, which is not very
likely in view of Jer 41.5, failure to mention the destruction
of the Temple of Jerusalem would suggest a date between 612
and 587/86. - It still could be argued that the old prayer
begins with v. 6, v. 5 being part of the later narrative.
While this is certainly true of 5a, a comparison with Ps 105
and 106, which are similar in character to our piece, shows that
historical retrospective prayers may well open with a conven-
tional praise of God. (Cmp. Ne 9.6 f. with Ps 105.7 for
further similarity of form. The pattern recurs in the Piyut

אמ‪י‬ץ כח [Ashkenazic _Avoda_ for the Day of Atonement].)

473   Such as 3.1b; 51.2.

474   50; 73-83.

475   42; 44-49; 84 f.; 87 f.

476   39; 62; 77 (together with אסף). אֵיתָן (89.1) may
be added, since the _heroes eponymoi_ are identical. A fine
explanation of the change of the names is given by G. von Rad,
Das Geschichtsbild des chronistischen Werkes (BWANT 54), 1930,
p. 112.

477   50; 73; 75-77; 79 f.; 82 f.

478   47-49; 84 f.; 87 f.

479   Cf. n. 476.

480   Some substantives, listed in Nos. 139 ff., as
well as others (e.g. שִׁיר) show that the psalms have full use
for synonyms of מזמור .

481   It is unsound to approach the explanation of art
terms by mere (and often doubtful) etymology; cf. B. Duhm,
Die Psalmen, 1899, p. XXXI. Knowing only the meaning of _tre_
or _fugare_, one would conceive of the "trio" (in a scherzo) as
of a three-part piece or of the "fugue" as of a war song sung
at, or commemorating, the pursuit of fleeing enemies.

482   16; 56-60.

483   Cf. the bibliography GB, p. 517; LVT, p. 630.
Further N.H. Torczyner, _Leshonenu_ 6 (1933 f.), pp. 120-126;
E. Zolli, mentioned by R. Tournay, RB 59 (1952), p. 442.

484   v. 19b. The frame is late.

485   42; 44-47; 49; 84 f.; 88.

486   75 f.; 80 f.

487   62 (cf. BH); 77.

488   How readily one would expect to find this frequent word in the psalms proper depends on the explanation he prefers. If it is taken as denoting an instrument, it would be grouped with the instruments, p. 63, and would be as acceptable to the psalms as they are. If it is taken as denoting a person, the occurrence of the infinitive לְנַצֵּחַ in 1 Ch 15.21 shows that the verb with its musical meaning is capable of a living conjugation and its use in the psalms would be conceivable.

489   32; 42; 44 f.; 52-55; 74; 78; 88 f.; 142.

490   78.

491   42; 44 f.

492   47.8 where this word is variously taken by ancient and modern interpreters as an adverbial expression (LXX, T, V) or a direct object (S). The explanation proposed here, with which one may compare the marginal remark הַגָּיוֹן (9.17), makes vv. 7 f. one tristich, each <u>stichos</u> of which closes with זַמֵּרוּ. Translation: "Yea, play to the King of the whole earth, to God !"

493   Depending on the inclusion or exclusion of שׁוֹפָר, מִנִּים צְלְצְלִים and עוּגָב.

494   Counting or not counting כְּלִי שִׁיר and its variants.

495   For various reasons, the possibility of further enlarging the contrasting sets has not been pursued here: neither by interpreting the absence in Chronicles and in related

passages of two items of psalm language for the Temple, viz.
21) סך (3:0) and 133)משכן , pl. in form...(5[4]:0 [sic], cf.
n. 179), nor by elaborating on the absence in the psalms proper
of the musical terms גאית עלמות (read probably עֲלָמִית) etc.,
occurring in the psalm headings and, one of them also, in
1 Ch 15.20 (cf. GuBe, pp. 455-458).

496   I √זמר:verb 24 times, musical instruments 9(13)
times, the balance 24 times.

497   If 150) עשור (or נבל עשור)is an instrument different from the usual נבל, then 144.9, a real vow in which the
prayer for salvation (vv. 5-8) culminates, would also formally
round out the picture.

498   P. 65.

499   Ne 12.27, 35 f., 41.

500   See E. Curtis, A Critical...Commentary on the
Books of Chronicles, 1910, p. 6.

501   R.H. Pfeiffer, Introduction to the O.T., 1941,
p. 811.

502   Post World War I reëditions of earlier books are
not surveyed.

503   JBL 40 (1921), pp. 104-124.

504   In Die Religion in Geschichte und Gegenwart I², 1927,
col. 1664; more explicitly so in REN, p. XXV.

505   In J.W. Rothstein-J.Hänel, Das erste Buch der
Chronik, 1927, p. LXIX, according to REN, p. XXV.

506   L. c. (n. 476). Von Rad as well as Sellin,

Oesterley, and Meinhold (see nn. 508-510) who follow him
speak of two Chroniclers. Sellin and Oesterley date the
second around 350 B.C. Von Rad does not explicitly date either,
but from the presentation of his case it becomes rather clear
that he belongs to the group of the early daters.

507   Die Althebräische Literatur, 1930, p. 184
("Anfänge...schwerlich vor Nehemia...Vollendung...erst in
einiger Entfernung von der Reform [Ezra's and Nehemiah's]
selbst").

508   Geschichte des israelitisch-jüdischen Volkes II,
1932, pp. 172 ff.

509   A History of Israel II, 1932, p. 141.

510   Einführung in das AT, 3rd ed., 1932, p. 303.

511   GuBe, p. 440.

512   Einleitung ins AT, 1934, p. 267, according to
REN, p. XXV.

513   Einleitung in das AT, 1934, p. 613.

514   Die Gesetze im Pentateuch, 1940, p. 67, n. 2.
Noth's study might not have been known to Pfeiffer.

515   See n. 506.

516   The Work of the Chronicler, 1939, pp. 56-63,
158, passim.

517   Von Moses bis Paulus, 1922, p. 505. Albright's
study, cf. n. 503, might not have been known to Kugler.

518   Both in E. Kautzsch[4]-A. Bertholet, Die Heilige
Schrift des AT II, 1923, pp. 500 and 564, respectively.

519   Geschichte des Volkes Israel III 2, 1929, p. 683.

520   An Introduction to the Books of the OT, 1934, p.112. This seems to be Robinson's opinion, since Oesterley held the other view shortly before, cf. n. 509, with no new argument being adduced in the later work.

521   In The Westminster Dictionary of the Bible, 1944, p. 101.

522   M.Ṣ. Segal, Mevoʾ hamiqraʾ (III), 1946 f., p. 801.

523   Oud-Israëlitische Geschriften, 1948, p. 238.

524   Überlieferungsgeschichtliche Studien I, 1943, pp. 192 ff.

525   Histoire de la littérature hébraïque et juive, 1950, p. 636.

526   In Harper's Biblical Dictionary, 1952, p. 99.

527   P. 66.

528   It is neither necessary nor advisable to go back beyond the fifth century B.C. If one were to assume that the changes from the pre-Exilic to the post-Exilic cult are responsible for the linguistic changes under discussion, he would deny the existence of post-Exilic psalms, and this is unlikely.

529   L. c. (n. 519), p. 659.

530   The problem of the order Ezra-Nehemiah or Nehemiah-Ezra does not affect our deliberations; cf. REN, pp. 70 f.

531   REN, pp. 171, 215.

532   REN, pp. 167, 212.

www.ingramcontent.com/pod-product-compliance
Lightning Source LLC
Chambersburg PA
CBHW050404110426
42812CB00006BA/1797

9 781666 729436